A Desert
in
the Ocean

The Spiritual Journey according to
St Brendan the Navigator

DAVID ADAM

PAULIST PRESS
New York/Mahwah, New Jersey

First published in Great Britain in 2000
Triangle
Society for Promoting Christian Knowledge
Holy Trinity Church
Marylebone Road
London NW1 4DU

ISBN 0-8091-3994-4

Published in North America by Paulist Press
997 Macarthur Boulevard
Mahwah, New Jersey 07430

www.paulistpress.com

Typeset in Plantin Light by
Pioneer Associates, Perthshire
Printed in Great Britain by
Caledonian International Ltd, Glasgow

Contents

Introduction

Life is meant to be an adventure. When we cease to reach out and stretch ourselves something in us dies or we feel frustrated; for life to be lived to the full it has to be adventurous. I believe that God calls us to adventure, to extend ourselves, and to seek new horizons. Our God is the God who makes all things new and he wants us to walk in newness of life. A relationship with God will extend our vision, our sensitivity and indeed our whole life. Whenever life gets static or dull God calls us out to risk and to be renewed.

> God our pilgrimage impels,
> To cross sea-waste or scale life-fells;
> A further shore,
> One hill brow more,
> Draws on the feet, or arm-plied oars,
> As the soul onward, upward soars.
> (McLean, 1961, p. 55)

I like reading adventure stories of men and women reaching out into the unknown. It is good to read of people getting themselves into totally new situations and wonder how you yourself would react. As I read Adamnan's *Life of Columba* I came across a statement, concerning an adventurer, that fascinated me:

> Cormac, grandson of Lethan, a truly pious man, who not less than three times went in search of a desert in the ocean but did not find it.

1

Adamnan writes that he did not find it because:

> he irregularly allowed to accompany him in the voyage a monk who is going away from his own proper abbot without obtaining his consent.
>
> (Reeves, 1874, Book 1 Chapter 6)

I discovered that the same Cormac made three attempts to find a 'desert in the ocean', and though he failed each time he did reach the Orkneys from Iona. In his last voyage to find the desert he went where no one had been before and experienced things that no one had experienced before:

> his voyage seemed to be extended beyond the limits of human wanderings and to return was impossible . . . Cormac who by sailing too far has passed the bounds of human enterprise and is exposed at this moment to dreadful alarm and fright, in the presence of monsters that were never before seen, and are almost indescribable.
>
> (Reeves, 1874, Book 2 Chapter 43)

Cormac was an adventurer indeed, but what captured my attention more was, 'he sought a desert in the ocean'. There is a sense of foolishness in the phrase that took my fancy. While most people are looking for oceans of wealth, seeking to fill empty spaces with things, here was someone going in the opposite direction. Cormac was not following the trend but going his own way. While people were seeking to amass possessions and become the centre of attention, here was a man willingly giving up all and going out into the unknown and, at the same time, facing many dangers. As so many were looking for an easy life, Cormac was stretching himself to his limits; he was giving up safety and security to venture into the unknown. Here was someone risking life and limb to find a place where he could serve his God. Cormac was, obviously, of a heroic mould and a most adventurous person. If asked why he did it, I am sure he would answer, 'For the love of God.'

My immediate reaction to Cormac was: 'He must be Irish, or at least Celtic.' Surely, it is only a race with such a sense of the 'beyond' or a sense of foolishness that would seek a 'desert in the ocean'. Then I remembered two heroes of the Celtic church, who are depicted on the High Cross of Ruthwell and on other high crosses in Ireland, St Antony of Egypt and St Paul of Thebes, the founding desert fathers. Above these two saints is usually carved a raven which brought daily bread to St Paul of Thebes and a double ration when St Antony visited him. The image of two men dependent on nature and sharing their resources in the desert told of a way of life that many in Ireland sought to copy.

The desert fathers and mothers moved away from wealth and status, away from a church that was becoming popular and growing in power; they moved out of the ocean of hyperactivity and self-justification into the stillness and silence of the desert. They left a people that was seeking to be settled for a life that would be full of adventure. These men and women were not running away from life or the world; they were choosing to enter more deeply into life and the world around them. They fled from the continual distractions and trivialities of their society and launched themselves into the deep and into the desert. They sought to leave behind pettiness and smallness of mind, the perpetual flitting from thing to thing; and to exchange it for seeking God in all things and to dedicate themselves fully to doing his will. They sought a great adventure, and no one who knows the desert can think it was an easy option. They may not have thought of changing the world but they were determined to change themselves; they were determined to die for something rather than of something, to show that life had depth, was adventurous and worth living.

Unless we seek to understand the 'desert tradition' that runs through Celtic spirituality we will not do justice to understanding their way of life and we may miss out on that which would enrich our lives; in fact the place where we experience our resurrection. The *Diseart De*, the 'Desert of God', may be a place of renunciation but it is also where the senses are heightened rather than dulled, where life is not settled but being forever extended. The call of the desert is a call to see beyond the obvious, to reach out for the invisible and to put our trust in our God. The desert is not a hiding place but a place where all is revealed. If the desert is a place of pruning, it is a pruning that life may blossom and grow in the right direction. It is not so much a return to the natural as to the supernatural, to discover the extra-ordinary that is ever present in the ordinary. The desert is the place where they sought to live life in the depths and in a constant relationship to the ever-present God. The Celtic Christians withdrew from a world that was blind to the presence and sought to live in the depths and wonder of God. A ninth-century Irish poem invites us all to withdraw and adore:

Let us adore the Lord,
The Maker of wondrous works,

4

> The great bright heaven and its angels,
> The white-waved ocean on earth.
>
> (Irish poem, ninth century)

For many the only way to be able to do this was to withdraw, at least for a little while, from what was absorbing them and concentrate on God and the 'otherworld' which was ever present.

The otherworld is always near to the Celtic mind and breaks into our world, allowing us to enter and enjoy it even now. There are not two separate worlds but the material and the spiritual are deeply interwoven in one: heaven and earth are one, and if we lose sight of one or the other we are not leading a fully human life. We may have to look for it, but the world beyond our world is ever also within it. A slight shift in where we stand and the world beyond reveals itself to us. Some sought a desert in the ocean so that they could live in the depth of God's presence. By placing themselves on the 'edge' of this world, they sought the chance to let the other world break through and to see both as one.

We often set boundaries that are unreal and in doing so close our eyes and our lives to the wonders that are about us. There is no easier way to become blind than to fill our hearts and minds with the trivial and the myopic pursuit of instant ease and pleasure. We need to capture the awareness of our own life as an adventure rather than just follow the adventure of others. I believe that whoever is called of God is called to adventure. This will demand that we make decisions and take action to do things that some might not understand but it would be well worth it, especially if we seek to do it for the love of God. We need to set ourselves time and space for this quest; perhaps it will

5

be necessary to seek our own desert in the ocean. The strange thing about the desert in the ocean is that it is not always necessary to travel to find it; more often it takes a change in ourselves than a journey through space.

At this stage you should begin by asking yourself if you want to go any further. Do you really want to launch out into the deep for the love of God? Are you ready to risk and adventure, to extend your life and put your faith in God? Are you truly ready to leave all for his love and to follow him? Have you heard the voice that asks you to seek a desert in the ocean? There is no doubt that God is calling you. He called you into being. He calls you to be found by him; know that him whom you seek has been seeking you and wanting you to open your life to him.

Some of the questions you may like to raise can be found in a poem which is often credited to St Brendan the Navigator, though in its present form it is of a much later date. The questions are addressed to God and to the poet himself. We will use this poem as a guide to our own call and adventure. We will look at extracts from the 'Voyage of Brendan' and relate them to our own situation. The chapters of this book will be comments on the poem and at the end of each chapter there will be a series of exercises and actions we can take. The whole idea is to discover our own desert in the ocean and look for the Promised Land which is there for those that are willing to venture. From the start we will be asked if we are willing to pay the cost. Are we ready to give up all for the hidden treasure, to seek until we discover the pearl of great price?

Dag Hammarskjöld in his book *Markings* encourages us to start with these words:

Once I answered Yes to Someone – or Something.
And from that hour I was certain that existence is
   meaningful,
and that, therefore, my life in self surrender has a
   goal.

(Dag Hammarskjöld, 1964, p. 169)

Brendan's Prayer on the Mountain

Shall I abandon, O King of Mysteries, the soft
   comforts of home?
Shall I turn my back on my native land, and my
   face towards the sea?

Shall I put myself wholly at the mercy of God,
   without silver, without horse, without fame and
   honour?
Shall I throw myself wholly on the King of kings,
   without sword and shield, without food and
   drink, without a bed to lie on?

Shall I say farewell to my beautiful land, placing
   myself under Christ's yoke?
Shall I pour out my heart to him, confessing my
   manifold sins and begging forgiveness, tears
   streaming down my cheeks?

Shall I leave the prints of my knees on the sandy
   beach, a record of my final prayer in my native
   land?
Shall I then suffer every kind of wound the sea
   can inflict?

Shall I take my tiny coracle across the wide,
   sparkling ocean?
O King of Glorious Heaven, shall I go of my own
   choice upon the sea?
O Christ will you help me on the wild waves?
                                    (van de Weyer, 1990)

The Call to Adventure

It was a cold winter's night and I had been allowed to go to the 'pictures' with a friend; the film that was showing was *Scott of the Antarctic*. My friend and I were spellbound, though I feel that it moved me most and in a powerful way. The men were such heroes and bore their troubles so bravely. I was amazed how they withstood the cold and the ice. I was touched by the going out of Captain Oates into the snow for I knew what he was doing and that he would not come back. He was giving up his life for his friends. When it was all over and my friend and I had parted ways, I stripped off my coat and jacket and let the cold get at me; my thin shirt was no protection from the frosty night air. By the time I got home I was thoroughly cold, though I had not noticed because I was having a great adventure. I got a good telling-off for not wearing my jacket or coat. As I put my hands around a warm cup of cocoa, I felt I had shared in a good adventure and had tried to live like a hero. It is important that life is lived with a sense of partaking in something bigger than ourselves.

A story that I heard in school and which also inspired me was about the first Bishop of Melanesia who had many adventures. I found one story from his boyhood particularly exciting. John Coleridge Patterson came down to breakfast one morning to hear his mother reading a letter from her cousin, a missionary bishop in the West Indies. The letter vividly described a hurricane and how it devastated a wide area. 'Well, Coley?' his mother asked, noticing that the lad had been deeply moved on hearing the letter. His swift reply was, 'I will be a bishop one day and I too will have a hurricane.' Later, at the age of 44, John Coleridge Patterson died as a martyr for Christ. He was the first Bishop of Melanesia and on his last journey his ship was mistaken for a slave ship and the natives attacked and killed him and his crew as they came ashore. He lived a life of adventure and fulfilled a calling that he first heard through a letter from a relative. In the end he even had his own personal hurricane in the attack of his ship.

Every now and again something happens in our lives to challenge us, or to make us change direction. We are going along minding our own business when suddenly it happens, and life is never the same again. For many people the highlight of this experience is when they meet their loved one for the first time and feel a great attraction; for others it is a visit to a special place or coming upon a new vision of something. At least once in our lives there is an event for which we would give up everything; such giving up is not sacrifice for it is the leaving of one thing for something better. To make such a move is not to deny ourselves but rather to find fulfilment in our newfound life; it is to reach out and extend ourselves. The call is often to awaken out of sleep and live fully in the present; it is to know that you have arrived and are where you should be. When we awaken, we arrive and become at home in the world and the world itself becomes presence-filled.

I was once travelling across France and Switzerland by train on my way to Austria. I wanted to be in the Alps. I awoke in Switzerland as the dawn was touching the tops of the Alps and making the snowy peaks all rosy. I had never seen such a sight. I had miles to go, but I knew I had already arrived; I was already in a different landscape. I was suddenly wide awake and absorbing as much as I could. Everything had a radiance and a glory that I had not seen before. I had awoken to a new day in a new world.

The saying 'the journey is more important than the arrival' must have been written for a tourist board. Such words fit well the consumer age that wants you never to arrive but ever to move on and to amass more and more. Although movement is necessary for life, to know when you have arrived is necessary for fulfilment. When you arrive you are suddenly awakened to new possibilities and new depths. Sometimes that awakening comes in a special way, although even then it is only possible if we have eyes to see.

One late August night the 16-year-old Cuthbert was watching over the sheep in the hills of Northumbria. It was a dark night. Suddenly he saw angels descending and ascending and taking a soul of exceeding brightness to heaven. The next day he would learn of Aidan's death. That night he awoke his companions and said:

> Alas, wretches that we are, who are given up to sleep and sloth and are not worthy to behold the glory of those servants of Christ who are ever watchful. For I myself, though I was watching in prayer for but a short part of the night, have nevertheless seen the wonders of God. The gate of heaven was opened and the spirit of a certain saint was conducted there with an angelic retinue: and while we dwell in utter darkness, he now, blessed for ever, beholds the glory of heavenly abode and Christ its King.
>
> (Colgrave, 1985, p. 167)

God is the God who comes and calls us again and again. If we are awake and alert we will hear him often. Vocation is not a one-off event; God does not just seek us out once, he calls and calls again, he is the God who calls. He is the God who called the world into being out of love, calling every individual into life and to share in his love. He called Abraham to go out into the unknown. He called Moses from the burning bush. He called Isaiah from the throne room in the Temple. God's call is not something that happens once and then it is finished with, for in calling he desires to have a loving relationship with us. If we keep our eyes, ears and hearts open we will hear his call many times. If the noise of the world seeks to drown it out we will need to create silence and space, our own desert in the ocean.

Celtic folk tales and legends are full of people hearing a call from beyond or from within. In the 'Voyage of Bran', the voyage begins with a vision and the rest of the story is the voyage to fulfil the vision and its call.

> One day, in the neighbourhood of the stronghold, Bran went about alone, when he heard music behind him. As often as he looked back, 'twas still behind him the music was. At last he fell asleep at the music, such was its sweetness. . . .

When he wakes up, a mysterious woman sings to him and the song was to disturb his way of living, it was a call to seek the 'beyond':

> There is a distant isle
> Around which sea-horses glisten:
> A fair course against the white-swelling surge . . .
>
> Glittering through beautiful ages,
> Lovely land throughout the world's age,
> On which many blossoms drop.
>
> An ancient tree there is with blossoms,
> On which the birds call the Hours.
> 'Tis in harmony is their wont
> To call together every Hour . . .

14

Without grief, without sorrow, without death,
Without any sickness, without debility.

Do not fall on a bed of sloth,
Let not intoxication overcome thee,
Begin a voyage across the sea.

(Meyer, 1895, p. 3)

Who could resist such a vision or challenge? The 'Voyage of Bran' is about Bran's travelling to that distant isle and visiting many other islands on the way. Bran is warned that idleness and intoxication are both dangers to the real adventure that life offers to him. He must step out from what others settle for and launch out into the deep. This challenge comes to us all in one way or another. It is all too easy to seek a settled existence and avoid anything that disturbs us. It is good to remember that it was the Spirit that drove Jesus into the desert, and that the same Spirit comes and disturbs our settled existence, calling us to adventure.

In the 'Song of Maelduin', about one of the great Celtic voyagers, we hear of his call to extend his life, to adventure and be willing to surrender himself. Such a call had to be answered speedily or the hearing of the call would fade. All the while there is this feeling that whoever lets go and sets out will find adventure; there is a bigger world for us all to explore and the possibilities of extending ourselves are endless. Suddenly, as if a fog has lifted we are given again the opportunity to reach beyond the visible.

THE SONG OF MAELDUIN

There are veils that lift, there are bars that fall,
There are lights that beacon, and winds that call —
Goodbye!

There are hurrying feet, and we dare not wait,
For the hour is on us – the hour of Fate,
The circling hour of the flaming gate –
Goodbye – goodbye – goodbye!

Fair, fair they shine through the burning zone –
The rainbow gleams of a world unknown:
Goodbye!
And oh! to follow, to seek, to dare,
When step by step in the evening air
Floats down to meet us the cloudy stair:
Goodbye – goodbye – goodbye!
The cloudy stair of the Brig o' Dread
Is the dizzy path our feet must tread –
Goodbye!
O children of time – O Nights and Days,
That gather and wonder and stand and gaze,
And wheeling stars in your lonely ways,
Goodbye – goodbye – goodbye!

The music calls and the gates unclose,
Onward and onward the wild way goes –
Goodbye!
We die in the bliss of a new birth,
O fading phantoms of pain and mirth,
O fading loves of the old green earth –
Goodbye – goodbye – goodbye!

(Rolleston, 1913, p. 37)

All at once something calls us and demands that we
say 'goodbye' to the life we have been living and set
out on a new course, 'to follow, to seek, to dare'. There
is a part of us that longs for such a call and that needs
to be stretched, and there is part of us that is afraid
to risk our safety and our security. We would like to
adventure but not to risk, but where there is no risk

there is no adventure. If we need to know where we are going, what we are doing and who will be meeting us, we run the risk of life becoming tedious and of being bored. It is no use having visions if we cannot work for their fulfilment. It is from entering new areas, having new experiences, reaching new heights and depths that we both learn and grow. It is no use talking of the 'Promised Land' unless we are willing to venture into the desert to reach it.

There is a lovely story in *The Anglo-Saxon Chronicle* of three Irishmen who landed in Cornwall after having crossed the sea in a boat made of hides and without oars. When they were asked in the presence of King Alfred of Wessex why they had come they replied, 'We stole away because we wanted for the love of God to be on pilgrimage, we cared not where.' The seeking of a desert in the ocean and the desire to go on pilgrimage for the love of God reflect the same yearning to extend one's life and to find not only meaning but one's true home. It is not surprising that the Irish, who lived on the 'edge of the world', were a nation who were forever reaching out into the beyond. In a sense, the beyond was always on their doorstep and now and again people were accidentally drawn into it. If people came from the 'back of beyond' with a story of what they had seen, adventurers would want to go there and even further. What the pilgrim seeks is not a new territory but a new spiritual depth, a beyond in our midst. Every true pilgrimage is not only an outward journey but a journey inwards and we all have great depths to discover within ourselves.

St Brendan the Navigator looked for a special island in the west for over seven years. He travelled not only over the sea but through the daily services and the liturgy of the church. Brendan not only landed on islands in the ocean but on church festivals throughout his journey; his was a journey of the spirit as well as across the Atlantic. God would call to him not only in new places but in revisiting the great moments in the life of Christ. Often we are not able to escape to a desert island but we can create our own. We can make a place in our home and in our heart where we are able to listen more attentively to the word of God. Adventurous living is not only going out, it is living in the depths of our being; it is expressed in how we respond to the word of God, how we react to the liturgy. If there is nothing in us that responds, we need to hear that as a call and seek to cure the emptiness within. We can let the church bell on Sunday – or the time of a service – become a call to God and respond positively to it and become aware once more of the presence in our midst. In the Celtic communities when the bell rang for the daily services all work stopped so that hearts and minds could be centred on their God. Today we need find something that would so direct us and encourage us to make a space for our God.

St Brendan was born at the 'edge of the world' in what is now County Kerry. His birthplace was near Tralee on the north side of the bay overlooking the Western Sea. There is no other land mass from there until you come to Labrador or Newfoundland. Brandon Mountain, near his home, overlooks the sea. On the landward side Lindberg landed the *Spirit of St Louis* in his historic crossing of the Atlantic. It is not surprising that adventuring in the sea and sailing was in Brendan's blood; he saw the ocean as a place to adventure and to reach out into the unknown.

Brendan was the founding father of the monastery of Clonfert, which was built on a bend of the River Shannon between Lough Derg and Lough Ree.

Clonfert means 'Meadow of Miracles' and it is here that one of Brendan's own kinsmen came with an account of the wonders he had seen on his voyage from over the seas. Barinthus told Brendan of how he went to visit his son Mernoc who had gone to live the life of a hermit on an island in the west. On the western shore of that desert in the ocean, Mernoc suggested he and his father got into a boat and went westwards to the island that is called the 'Promised Land of the Saints', where night never falls and days have no ending. Mernoc told how he stayed in the Promised Land of the Saints for two full weeks without the need for food or drink. Something in Brendan reacted to this story; it was the call of God to adventure, the call to go out on the sea and into the unknown. Brendan heard a whisper, a voice that spoke in secret, and he knew life would never be the same again. From the back of beyond had come this call to go out over the edge of the world and into the unknown. He heard that there is a land beyond what he had known, a horizon beyond the known horizon. A voice from within him seemed to call; it asked if he should go, and he knew that he must.

The morning after Barinthus left, Brendan, without delay, chose 14 monks from the community and closed himself up with them in a place of prayer. He said to them, 'My most beloved co-warriors in spiritual conflict, I beg you to help me with your advice, for I am consumed with a desire so ardent that it casts every other thought and desire out of my heart. I have resolved, if it be God's will, to seek out that Land of Promise.' To a man, the 14 said they would like to go with Brendan. 'We are prepared to go with you no matter what the consequences may be. We seek to do one thing alone – the will of God.'

It is important that in heeding any call we test out as best we can that it is God's call and not just some fantasy of our own. We need to share with friends who understand and are believers, we need to seek that it is the will of God. For the desert fathers and the Celtic Christians the story of Abraham leaving Ur of the Chaldees became an image and model for doing God's will and adventure. The following is said to be part of a sermon by St Columba:

> God counselled Abraham to leave his own country and go in pilgrimage into the land which God had shown him, to wit the 'Land of Promise' – Now the good counsel which God had enjoined here on the father of the faithful is incumbent on all the faithful, that is to leave their country and their land, their wealth and their worldly delight for the sake of the Lord of the Elements, and go in perfect pilgrimage in imitation of Him.
>
> (Chadwick, 1961, p. 64)

We all must seek out places and times when we can be quiet and wait upon our God, for God calls us today as he called us yesterday. We do not have to go far for God is with us, though we might have to step out of the familiar to hear 'the still small voice'.

> Come in, let us bow, prostrate ourselves,
> and kneel in front of the Lord our maker,
> for this is our God,
> and we are the people of his pastures,
> the flock that he guides.
> If only you would listen to him today,
> 'Do not harden your hearts . . .'
>
> (Psalm 95.6–8)

EXERCISES

Pray slowly and attentively:

> Lord, open my ears to your call.
> make me attentive to you.
> Open my eyes to your presence,
> make me aware of you.
> Open my heart to your love.

THE 5P EXERCISE

A favourite exercise of mine is the 5P exercise. I use this as a way of creating space and waiting upon my God. It is called 5P because each part of the exercise begins with an action starting with the letter P:

> Pause, Presence, Picture, Ponder, Promise

Pause

It is important to stop and let go of what you are doing. Give yourself a break from activity and justification by works. Let go and let God have a chance to speak. Remember God speaks most to those who can keep silent. Let the stopping be not only of words and actions; let it be a stilling of your heart, mind and body. Do a check over your body, is it relaxed? Let go of all tension out of your hands, feet, neck, be still and at ease. Let your mind relax; you may need a word or a sentence to help you do this.

Say quietly, 'Come, Lord God, I am open to you', and repeat it with each breath.

Breathe deeply . . . slowly . . . comfortably.

'Come, Lord, I am open to you.'

Be still . . .

Presence

Know that God is with you and speaks to you.

21

This is the reason for creating this space, not for knowledge, not even for peace, or for love, but for God himself who comes to you. (No doubt you will then receive his gifts also.) God is with you. Open yourself to the presence. Seek to be aware of the great mystery of God that is about you. God will not force himself upon you, you need to open to him. You cannot imagine the Presence or create it, for it is there, but you can open your life to him.

Try and relax in the Presence as you would in the sun on a nice day.

You can say quietly: 'You Lord are . . . You Lord are here . . . You Lord are with me . . . You Lord are seeking me . . . You Lord are . . . You Lord . . . You. I open myself to you.

Picture
Read Genesis 12.1–9. Picture the calling of this old man. Abram and his wife Sarai were elderly. Abram was at the stage when most people would think their time of adventure was well over; he was 75. He was well settled, comfortable, prosperous. He had reasonable security and safety in his home surroundings. From all this God called Abram, to leave his safety and comfort and to move into the unknown. No doubt Sarai had something to say. Try and picture this old couple setting out into the unknown with hearts of faith.

Ponder
Think how you would have reacted to such a call. Do you in fact hear God's call today? By faith Abraham when called to go to a place he would later receive as his inheritance, obeyed and went, even though he did not know where he was going (Hebrews 11.8).

Sometimes the call is not clear. It is expressed only

in a discontent with the present, with the awareness that life and our surroundings, if not the world, could be better than they are. There is always an immediacy about the call; once heard it should not be put off. We are asked to respond like Isaiah and say, 'Here am I, Lord, send me.' There is a need to know that the call comes from beyond us; it is God's call and God's will, not just a whim or a desire of our own. Seek to discover what Jesus meant when he said, 'You did not choose me, no, I chose you' (John 15.16). This can be the wonderful beginning of an exciting adventure.

Promise
Those whom God calls he sends. The call to move out and adventure is of its nature exciting. Too often after the call nothing happens. Promise to keep at least a little of each day open to God and say each day, 'Here I am, Lord, send me.'

OFFER YOURSELF TO GOD

Father, I abandon myself into your hands;
do with me what you will.
Whatever you may do, I thank you;
I am ready for all, I accept all.
Let only your will be done in me,
and in all your creatures.

I wish for no more than this, O Lord.
Into your hands I commend my soul;
I offer it to you with all the love of my heart,
for I love you, Lord,
and so need to give myself,
to surrender myself into your hands,
without reserve and with boundless confidence.
For you are my Father.

(De Foucauld, 1977)

Moving Out

I must admit I hate moving. I like to be settled and to enjoy the place I am in. When I was asked to leave my last parish and to move to Holy Island it bothered me intensely. I love the North Yorkshire Moors, their heather-clad hills and their moorland people. I had many friends and liked the churches I worked in. I had been there 23 years and thought I would spend the rest of my ministry there. If anyone had asked me I would have said, 'I intend to stay here always.' It was not to be, God once again called. He worked through various people and events to bring me towards Holy Island. Then a telephone call from the Bishop of Newcastle offering me the parish of Holy Island totally upset my ability to be settled. I became less at home where I was and began to look towards Holy Island. I shared this with my wife Denise and we decided together that we needed to look at the newly offered parish. We looked, we talked, we discussed it with a few friends, we prayed much, and slowly decided that this was the way we were being called. Friends said they could see God at work and it was his will. I only wished I could see more clearly.

The call of God demands of us a response. If we have any vision at all it demands of us a reaction. Having heard of the 'Land of Promise' and having chosen his men, Brendan sought to prepare them for their journey. They would have much to do and they must get their priorities right, so they observed a series of three-day fasts to cover the period of 40 days before they were due to set out. This witnessed that their priority above all else was God and his will.

When describing how a monk should please God, Columbanus said in a sermon: 'What is the best thing in the world? To please the Creator. What is his will? to fulfil what he commanded, that is, to live rightly and dutifully to seek the Eternal; for duty and justice are the will of Him who is dutiful and right.'
(Walker, 1970, p. 73)

In a catechism that is attributed to St Ninian we learn of the deep desire to do God's will.

NINIAN'S CATECHISM

Question	What is best in this world?
Answer	To do the will of our Maker.
Question	What is his will?
Answer	That we should live according to the laws of his creation.
Question	How do we know those laws?
Answer	By study – study the Scriptures with devotion.
Question	What tool has our Maker provided for this study?
Answer	The intellect which can probe everything
Question	And what is the fruit of study?
Answer	To perceive the eternal Word of God reflected in every plant and insect, every bird and animal, and every man and woman.

(van de Weyer, 1990, p. 96)

Brendan may say, 'I am resolved to do it if it is God's

will', but how are we to discern God's will? We should use all our faculties in seeking to do what God wants us to do but we would still be safer with some outside guidance also. Too often people have sought to go their own way and said, 'It is the will of God.' It is often necessary to test what we believe is God's will against the wisdom and guidance of other godly people. Brendan not only prayed with his co-warriors in Christ, he went to visit a monk called Enda who was on an island to the west. Brendan and his monks stayed on that island three days and nights seeking guidance and the blessing of St Enda. Above all it was important that God's will is sought and obeyed. More than one group of seekers for a desert in the ocean have failed because they were not setting out with the aim of doing the will of God. It was suggested Cormac failed in his desire for a desert in the ocean because he had on board those that were pleasing themselves rather than seeking the will of God.

Each day we must learn to say, 'Your will be done.' Celtic Christians often prayed these few lines that expressed their desire to do God's will, to die to self and to live for God:

> May we do the will of God
> Sharing in the death of Christ,
> Rising with him to eternal life.

For most of us, it is not lack of vision that holds us back, nor is it lack of resources; it is our own volition, our will power. It is not that we make a choice to do something else; it is that we fail to choose. What is of the uttermost importance to us who have the freedom of choice is that we make a choice, that we decide for ourselves to start the journey and to decide the direction we are going. The strange thing about this decision is that it is a way we already know, for God has already spoken of it to us in our heart. We need not fear that we will be diminished by seeking his will, in him life is ever moving and expanding. We should not kill our sensitivities for that would destroy our humanity. Like Jesus, we must come out of the desert with our senses heightened and guarded against temptation and fantasy. At all times God calls us to be fully alive and alert.

It is not enough to enter the desert. We need move forward to the Promised Land. We are a pilgrim people and 'strangers upon earth'. The first step is the hardest for it is to make the choice of the direction God wants us to go. It has been said that the hardest part of any journey is taking the first step. Choice is about commitment and about determination. Choice involves an act of volition; we are to use our will power. As Christians the decision is to say, 'Your will be done.'

There is an old fable of a donkey that starved to death because it could not make up its mind. One day when the farmer was going away he went to the donkey's stable and left it two bales of hay within its reach, one on its right and the other on its left. Then the owner of the donkey left it on its own for a while. The donkey saw two lovely bales of hay and could not decide which to eat first. Should it be the one on the right or the left? It found it hard to decide and dithered between the left and the right. The poor old donkey could not make up its mind and starved to death with food easily at hand. Too often we fail to move ahead because we do not make any definite decision. In a poem called 'Bees in Amber' John Oxenham wrote:

To every man there openeth
A way and ways and a way.
And the high soul treads the highway,
And the low soul gropes the low,
And in between on misty flats
The rest drift to and fro.
But to every man there openeth
A high way and a low,
And every man decideth
The way his soul should go.

(Oxenham, unsourced)

We decide whom or what we will serve and whom we
will become by the choices we make or do not make.
If we make comfort and money our goal we will put
our energies and abilities into these enterprises. We
will measure our life by how much comfort we have
achieved and how much money we have collected. If
we make the will of God our goal, we will be called
to adventure upon adventure; we will not be saved
from the troubles of this world but we will know who
goes with us and cares for us, for our God does not
leave us. We cannot start, we cannot set out until we
decide to do so. A Celtic prayer for the start of the day
and which Celtic Christians often said together on the
shore before they started the day's tasks says:

'Tis God's will I would do,
My own will I would rein:
Would give to God his due,
From my own due refrain;
God's path I would pursue,
My own path disdain.

(McLean, 1961, p. 59)

The call to move out comes seven times every day to a monk at the tolling of a bell. Seven times a day he is called to stop whatever he is doing and turn his thoughts and his heart to God. No matter what his work is, as soon as the bell rings he is expected to stop; no matter how important his task, God is to be given the priority. The saying of the Hours and the celebrating of the Holy Communion are a moving out of ordinary space and moving into another dimension. The saying of daily prayers is a daily steeping ourselves in eternity and in our God who is all about us.

In the case of Brendan, he and his monks would travel for seven years through the daily offices and the church seasons as well as over the ocean. The whole of the Brendan voyage is a deepening of awareness and spirituality, so it is no ordinary journey. It is not just into the deep of the sea but into the depths of God. This entering into the depths of God helps to account for the returning to the same place each year for seven years. On his journey to the Land of Promise, Brendan did not plot a straight course but rather a spiralling journey which returned to the same places for the major festivals. Nor is it accidental that the resting places have something to do with the festivals. At the Passover time, Maundy Thursday to the Easter Vigil, Brendan and his companions spent the time on the Island of Sheep. Easter was spent on the back of the great fish that rises from the deep. Pentecost was spent on the Island of Birds. St Peter's Day was spent on the ocean. Each place prepared them for the next stage of their journey. These men were travelling through the liturgy on a voyage of discovery and every time they returned to where they had been before they discovered something new. To view the daily services and the festivals in this way is to see that we can soon have our own 'deserts in the ocean'. By choice and effort we can step out of time and into eternity. This will demand that we are truly alert and ever watchful. To view each festival as a landing place and a stepping stone to the Promised Land is to have our liturgical calendar and festivals enriched as well as our lives.

Life seems to have lost a dimension for many people and so they are hardly alive in a world that is not fully alive. There is a great need to be in touch with what is around us and that includes the presence of our God. On the sea there is no room for the unaware, there has to be a constant watching of the wind and waves, a reckoning by the sun and stars. It is important to make sure you are on course and not just drifting with the current. There has to be a constant care of the vessel for on this all life depends. A voyage of discovery is not just a rowing about, it is about being open and aware. Each day will bring new adventures to those with eyes to see; there will be new depths and new horizons. No matter where we travel there will always be a beyond and a new horizon. The greatest danger to our journey is distraction, that is, anything that makes us lose contact with our true self and what is going on in the world around us. On the ocean of life distraction can lead to danger and to death. If we lose contact with wonder and mystery we become insensitive and therefore dangerous to ourselves and others. No matter what our age we need to continue to be aware and moving or we begin to die. Adventure and moving is a sign of life:

Old men ought to be explorers
Here and there does not matter
We must be still and still moving
Into another intensity

For a further union, a deeper communion
Through the dark cold and the empty desolation,
The wave cry, the wind cry, the vast waters
Of the petrel and the porpoise. In my end is my
    beginning.
(T. S. Eliot, 'East Coker', in Four Quartets, 1944)

In all our lives there are mystery and depths that are
unfathomable; if we lose our sight of this, life becomes
more of a problem or we become dull and bored.
Liturgy calls us into depths, to mystery and to create
our own desert in the ocean. Life and liturgy have
their special seasons: there are times of preparation for
great events, then the great events themselves and
there is the extension of that event for a season. Each
year something new is added to the pattern that comes
around once more. The major festivals should interpret
our life and our life interpret the festivals until all of
life becomes a celebration and an opening up to glory.
We need pay special heed to the times of preparation,
like Advent and Lent, if we are to get the fullness out
of Christmas and Easter. We need also keep the days
of the Christmas and Easter seasons if we are to enter
the experience in any depth. This will ask us each day
to thrust out a little from what we are doing and abide
in the mighty acts of God. We need to heed the slogan
that says, 'Christmas is not for a day, it is for life.'

As we live in a society that has lost the ability to
celebrate in any depth we are left with the instant and
the quick fix, the immediately visible and the present
reaction. If this was a true way of living in the present
it would be a wonderful experience but somehow it
leaves us thirsting after the next experience and a new
excitement. Our movement forward has little rhythm
and tends to be a spastic jerky movement that expends

much energy for little reward. We need to make space in our lives, preparation time, where we can relax and be with our God. We need to leave room after our words to enjoy the presence and the power of God in what we celebrate. If such a rhythm becomes part of our life we become rich indeed and we begin to discover wonder upon wonder. Daily prayer is not so much words but awareness, not so much a telling God but a being with him with all our senses alert to what God desires of us. Prayer is an entering fully into the Eternal that is all about us. The events that we look forward to in the liturgical seasons are always part of us and can come to be realized as our heritage at any time. Our lives and the great mysteries of the universe, the mystery of God himself are all interwoven like some great Celtic carpet pattern, with each thing touching and being part of another. We can experience at any moment what Gerard Manley Hopkins says of the world in his poem 'God's Grandeur':

The world is charged with the grandeur of God,
It will flame out, like shining from shook foil;
It gathers to a greatness, like ooze of oil
Crushed. Why do men then now not reck his rod?
Generations have trod, have trod, have trod;
And all is seared with trade: bleared, smeared with
    toil;
And wears man's smudge and shares man's smell:
    the soil
Is bare now, nor can foot feel, being shod.

And for all this, nature is never spent;
There lives the dearest freshness deep down
    things . . .

(Hopkins, 1972)

33

Never believe that the world or humankind has lost its glory, the presence of God has not left it. The glory may be somewhat tarnished but it is there and awaits to be revealed. If we follow the crowds, if we fill our lives with sounds, we may never see, hear or be aware of the wonder and glory. If we thrust out a little each day, making time and space, there are great wonders to behold. If we have lost all sense of glory it is time we moved and sought to reawaken our senses. Pelagius invites us:

Look at the animals roaming the forest: God's spirit dwells within them.

Look at the birds flying across the sky: God's spirit dwells within them.

Look at the tiny insects crawling in the grass: God's spirit dwells within them.

Look at the fish in the river and the sea: God's spirit dwells within them.

There is no creature on earth in whom God's spirit is absent.

Travel the ocean to the most distant land, and you will find God's spirit in all the creatures there.

Climb up the highest mountain, and you will find God's spirit among the creatures who live at the summit. When God pronounced that his creation was good it was not only that his hand had fashioned every creature, it was that his breath had brought every creature to life.

Look, too, at the great trees of the forest; look at the wild flowers and the grass in the field, look even on your crops, God's spirit is within all plants as well. The presence of God's spirit in all living beings is what makes them beautiful:

and if we look with God's eyes nothing on earth is ugly.

(van de Weyer, 1995, p. 71)

This discovery of the presence of God is to see all things in their depth and in their beauty. If we ignore the presence that vibrates in every atom then we live a lie, we become lonely and alone with a deep sense of loss. If everyone around us shares that same loss we are in danger of accepting that blindness for normality. The call to thrust out a little is a call to become more sensitive. It will ask us for a while to turn our back on our normal routine until we can become more sensitive. We need move from our activity into times of solitude and silence. Albert Camus, the French existentialist, said:

> To understand the world, it is necessary sometimes to turn away from the world: to serve men better, it is necessary for a moment to keep them at a distance.

(Camus, 1954, p. 13)

Let us ask with Brendan: 'Shall I turn my back on my native land, and my face towards the sea?'

EXERCISES

PRAY

I open my life to you Lord,
I make space in this day for your coming
I move from busyness to your stillness
I move from sounds to your silence
I move from insensitivity to awareness.
I thrust out from the land and look to heaven.

I open my life to you.
I open my heart to your love.
I open my ears to your call
I open my eyes to your presence
I open my life to you.

READ

Read Luke 5.1–11.
Picture the fishermen leaving their work. They put
down their netting needles. They bundle up their nets.
They stand on their feet and move out of the crowd.
See yourself moving out with them. Stop doing what
you are doing and move towards Jesus. Now they get
into the boat and push out just a little from the land.
For a moment they had their backs to the crowd and
were facing the sea; seek to enter the presence this
way. This would normally be the time for them to go
home and rest. It is restful in the boat. The waves are
very gentle and the rhythmic movement soothing. Jesus
speaks to the people and you are specially privileged
for you are near to him – but be warned he may ask
you to launch out into the deep with him and to do
what seem impossible things. It seems with Jesus there
is often this sequence: 'Come, be with me. Thrust out
a little from the land. Launch out into the deep. Do
what I ask. Follow me.' Think over how this sort of
pattern is at work in your life.

THINK OVER THESE WORDS

We are the music makers,
And we are the dreamers of dreams,
Wandering by lone sea-breakers,
And sitting by desolate streams:
World losers and world forsakers,
On whom the pale moon gleams;

Yet we are the movers and shakers
Of the world forever, it seems.

(O Shaughnessy, 1913, p. 1)

You seek the Lord? Seek, but only within yourself.
He is not far from anyone. The Lord is near to all
who truly call upon Him. Find a place in your
heart, and speak there with the Lord. It is the Lord's
reception room. Everyone who meets the Lord
meets him there; He has fixed no other place for the
meeting of souls.

(Theopan the Recluse)
(Ware, 1966, p. 187)

When you retreat into yourself, you should stand
before the Lord and remain in His presence, not
letting the eyes of the mind turn away from the
Lord. This is the true wilderness – to stand face to
face with the Lord.

(Theopan the Recluse)
(Ware, 1966, p. 81)

Into the Deep

Shall I put myself at the mercy of God?

This is a strange question for in reality we are all at the mercy of God every moment of our existence. Without God we would cease to exist, with God we survive and live in eternity. God in his mercy and goodness gives us life, gives us love, gives us himself. In return God asks us to give our love, our lives, ourselves to him. St Augustine expresses this in the prayer:

> Lord to turn away from you is to fall.
> To turn to you is to rise.
> To stand before you is to abide forever.
> (Augustine)

The question is posed by Brendan as he is about to set sail for a land he knows not where. Like many other Celtic sailors, Brendan is to become a pilgrim for the love of God. Brendan knows it is not an easy journey and he will need all the resources he can muster. He is going out into the unknown, where there is little to guide him, and not much protection. Brendan's belief in the Almighty, in his presence and love will give him courage and strength to journey and to go into the unknown. With St Paul, Brendan would affirm, 'Nothing can separate us from the love of God' in Christ Jesus (Romans 8.38–39). Time and again Brendan would seek to remind his companions of the presence and the love of God. In the journey through life, we are able to cope in the fair times and the bright times, but what about the storms? Our faith might be small but as long as it is in an Almighty God and a merciful God we should be able to venture. We need to know of the mercy of God, of his deep love and concern for us and this will give us both courage and hope.

Brendan set off at the time of the summer solstice; the wind was fair and they needed to do no more than steady their sails. Like most of life, the easy time suddenly disappeared; the sailors had to work hard to travel, they rowed and rowed until their strength failed. Now Brendan spoke to encourage them, 'Have no fear. God is our helper. He is our captain and guide and will steer us out of danger. Just leave the sails and let him do as he will with his servants in their boat.' The crew believed that with a good helmsman, meaning their God, they would weather the storms, triumph over the elements and reach their destination safely. The crew ate sparingly every day at the time of their evening prayers. After 40 days they found themselves without food. Then, one day, an island came into sight to the south of them. At first, they could find no harbour at which to land because of the cliffs, and it took them three days to find an entrance big enough for their boat. On the shore they met a dog which led them to a place where there was food and drink for them. Brendan gave thanks saying, 'Let us praise the God of heaven who gives every creature its food.'

There was no doubt in Brendan's mind that God had brought them safely this far and God would lead them on. God in his great mercy cares for his people. God's mercy is not just about forgiveness; it is about his loving relationship with his people. To put our trust in the mercy of God is to express what we feel about his nature. We can venture because we have a Father who loves us, cares for us, and will not let us perish. We can face the storms of life because our God is mightier than all the storms and will bring us safely home even if we fail to reach the harbour where we had hoped to arrive. He will bring us to his haven of rest.

Another time when Brendan and his companions were returning to the island where they had celebrated Maundy Thursday, they were so joyful that they rowed with all the strength they could muster. Brendan told them that they were not to be so foolish as to use up all their strength and tire themselves out. 'Is not the Lord our captain and helmsman? Leave it to him and he will direct us where he wills.' If this was a liturgical island and they were returning to the time of the Last Supper and Passion the message was still the same, 'Do not be in a rush, let God guide you. Put yourself under the guidance and mercy of God.' We need learn we will not enter into the Land of Promise or even into the fullness of the events of the calendar in our own might; we need the power of God to guide us. We will not be saved by our own strength or by speed but by the might and love of God. The power of God, the Spirit of God, is often symbolized by the wind. If we need direction and guidance in Bible reading or meditation, we need to seek the help of the Spirit of God. In our journey through life we are always dependent on the love and mercy of our God. The God whom we seek comes to meet us and assist us.

On another occasion Brendan and his companions had sailed for 40 days. Suddenly from behind them came a great sea monster of gigantic proportions. It was coming at great speed and looked as though it would devour them. The sailors were terrified. Knowing their own weakness they yelled, 'Good Lord, deliver us. Do not let the beast swallow us up.' Brendan, well-versed in the Scriptures, said to them, 'Do not be afraid, O you of little faith. God has always cared for us, he will save us now from the hands of this monster and from all perils that are to come.' The monster continued to pursue them and great waves buffeted the boat. The monks became more afraid than ever. Brendan lifted his hands in prayer and prayed, 'Lord, as you delivered David from the hand of Goliath, deliver us. Lord, as you delivered Jonah from the belly of the great whale, deliver us.' As Brendan was finishing his prayer another sea monster appeared and attacked the first one, and so the sailors were rescued. For those with eyes to see, God works his wonders and miracles through the world in which we live.

Whatever we make of these stories, they were told to affirm the love and the care of God for his people, that God does not want his loved ones to perish. These stories were told to show the power of prayer and that when we are weak we can come to God for strength; when we are in danger we should seek his help and protection. There is no doubt that the love and mercy of God are ever offered to us. As we live in a world that has little recourse to God, we may find this hard to accept. It must be remembered that the early Christian adventurers were no fools; they did not tempt providence or God, they did not take risks just to prove God's power. They were, however, willing to do their best and then leave the outcome to God and his mercy. They were sure that God would not leave them nor forsake them. Their pilgrimage is not only 'for the love of God' but in and into the love of God.

In listening to the Brendan stories it is good to remember that the sea to the west of Ireland was unexplored territory. Brendan's voyages were the 'space adventures' of their times. Like all good adventures there is a goal and there are experiences on the way. Even in modern space stories we expect the resources of the heroes to combat the evil they meet on their journeys. Brendan could hope to survive whatever the sea threw at him because he believed that God cared and would give him whatever is needed to travel through life. If Brendan had to describe this care and protection in a phrase he would talk of 'the mercy of God'.

In the early litanies there are many with the refrain 'Forgive' but the ones with 'Have mercy upon us' I feel are fuller and richer in their content as they reflect more than forgiveness, they tell of the love and compassion of God. There is a wonderful litany from the tenth century that is thought to have come from Iona; after each line we should add the refrain 'Have mercy upon us'.

Have mercy upon us,
O God the Father Almighty, God of hosts,
High God, O Lord of the world,
O ineffable God, O Creator of the Elements,
O invisible God, O incorporeal God,
O God beyond judgement, O impassible God,
O incorruptible God, O immortal God,
O immoveable God, O eternal God,
O perfect God, O merciful God,
O wondrous God, O dreadful God,
O God of the earth, O God of fire,
O God of the excellent waters
O God of the tempestuous and rushing air,
O God of the many languages round the circuit
    of the earth,
O God of the waves from the bottomless house
    of the ocean,
O God of the constellations, and all the bright stars,

O God who didst fashion the mass, and didst
  inaugurate day and night,
O God who didst rule over hell, and its rabble host,
O God who dost govern with archangels,
O golden good.
O heavenly Father who art in heaven
Have mercy upon us.

(Plummer, 1992, p. 79)

This litany has two further parts addressed to the Son
and the Holy Spirit as this is addressed to the Father.
There is something very powerful about saying a
litany like this while walking about or travelling. There
is great strength in affirming the love and compassion
of God throughout all of his creation. Time and again
we need remind ourselves that to ask for mercy is to
ask for God's love to be at work in our lives. We all
need to become pilgrims for the love of God, reaching
out to experience his mercy and protection.

Sometimes when words fail, I shorten the litany to
'Jesus Christ, Son of God, have mercy upon me'. This
does not diminish what I want to say but rather it
heightens it. In this short form the prayer is known as
the 'Jesus Prayer' and I first came across it while I was
at theological college. I was told that many Orthodox
Christians used this prayer as part of their daily worship and in fact some used only this prayer, repeating
it over and over. I could not believe that such a simple
sentence could have such depth, but then I did not
know that words could be used as gates to enter into
the depths of God's presence. For a long time I ignored
the Jesus Prayer and it was not part of my regular
prayer life. Then in 1972 I read the *The Way of a
Pilgrim* which is the story of a man who sought to pray
without ceasing and used the Jesus Prayer to achieve

his goal. Slowly, I discovered that this prayer is not so much about what is said but to whom it is said and his response to us.

The Jesus Prayer is about a living and loving relationship with our Lord. At its lowest level, though this is also its deepest level, it affirms or assumes that our Lord is always there: his presence never leaves us nor forsakes us. If we turn to our God with all our heart and mind and strength he awaits us. I was gradually learning that no one calls upon him that has not been called by him. To put ourselves wholly at his mercy is to accept his presence and the love He has for us. I spent some time with each word of the Jesus Prayer and let it vibrate in my life; I used the words to give myself to him who is present and gives himself to me. I sought him as my Lord and my Saviour, knowing that in his love and mercy he was seeking me out. To refuse to seek his mercy is to risk travelling alone, in our own puny strength and our own limited resources; it is to believe we can go it alone when the sea is so large and our boat so small. The Jesus Prayer has brought me through personal storms and dangers when I could find no other words. To be able to utter his name and trust in his mercy gives new hope and new light. In these few words I am able to affirm that I belong to God and I am loved by God.

In the services of the church when I say 'Lord have mercy, Christ have mercy, Lord have mercy', I do not narrow these words down to an asking of forgiveness – that is included but I seek all that the love and presence of God offers. Here in few words are the great riches of the gospel. To discover the mercy of God is to know we are ransomed, healed, restored and forgiven; above all it is to know that God gives himself to us in love.

God's mercy is often revealed in his protection and his delivering us from the powers of darkness. In the times of Brendan, there was a belief that the world was full of unseen forces for good and for evil. There was a great fear that the demons of the night or the air could attack at any time. Sometimes we have much more scientific names for what Brendan would have seen as demons but it does not mean we escape from the experience. We all have times when we feel that the powers about us seem to be against us. It is then we need to know our God is a loving merciful God who does not want us to perish but to have and enjoy everlasting life. One of my favourite passages comes from Isaiah:

Do not be afraid for I have redeemed you; I have called you by your name, you are mine. Should you pass through the sea, I will be with you; or through rivers, they will not swallow you up. Should you walk through the fire, you will not be scorched and the flames will not burn you. For I am the Lord, your God, the Holy One of Israel, your saviour.

(Isaiah 43.1–2)

In the same way Brendan seeks to express God's care and love to his weary companions by saying, 'God is our helper. He is our captain and guide and will steer us out of danger. Just leave the sails and let him do as he wills with his servants in their boat.' God's mercy will be revealed to them in his care for them. No doubt there were certain Bible passages in the mind of Brendan. In the stilling of the storm, the disciples were all at sea and Jesus was asleep in their boat. Now this is a situation I see very often. People are struggling against the storms of life; they say they believe in

46

Jesus, they even say they believe in his presence, but they let him sleep. In their troubles people forget to call upon him. In most lives it would seem that Jesus sleeps. We need to have the courage to awaken him, to call upon him, and to allow him to be active in our lives. We can call out as Oscar Wilde calls in his poem 'E Tenebris':

Come down, O Christ, and help me! reach thy hand,
For I am drowning in a stormier sea
Than Simon on the lake of Galilee.

(Wilde, 1998)

This is a reference to the other great storm story of Jesus and his disciples. This time, Jesus has sent the disciples ahead in the boat while he remains on the shore on a hillside to pray on his own. During the night crossing of Galilee, a storm arises. Jesus is aware that his friends are in danger and goes to them in the storm, walking in the storm itself and on the waves. As he approaches, the disciples cannot believe it is Him. This is not surprising, really! Who is it that can survive in the sea like that? With a growing awareness that it is Jesus, Peter says those wonderful words, 'Lord, if it is you, tell me to come to you.' As always Jesus says, 'Come.' With his eyes on Jesus, Peter seems able to walk the waves. Taking his eyes off Jesus, Peter notices the storm about him and he begins to sink. At this point Jesus reaches down and raises Peter and brings him to safety.

Whatever you make of this story, I have survived storms of life because of the presence and the strength of Jesus. When I am unable to cope alone I have put my trust in his mercy and I know he has uplifted me. In my ministry to other people, I see many who are beset by great waves and storms and who survive the ordeal and even walk tall because they are able to trust in the presence and in the mercy of God. Let us learn to be travellers in the love and mercy of our God.

EXERCISES

PRAY

Learn to pray the Jesus Prayer

Lord Jesus Christ, Son of God, have mercy upon me.

Make it your only prayer for about quarter of an hour each day for a while. Do not be afraid of such few words; learn their depth and use them with devotion.

READ

Read the story of Bartimaeus in Mark 10.46–52.

Pause

Close your eyes and know that though you cannot see it the world is still there. Know that God is present though you cannot see him. Be still in his presence. Seek to be sensitive to Him.

Picture

Picture the blind Bartimaeus sitting by the roadside begging. He cannot see but he can hear, and he is sensitive to movement. He hears that something different is going on, for the crowd is reacting in a different way. He asks what is happening and is told, 'Jesus of Nazareth is passing by.' Now that is too good an opportunity to miss. Listen to him shout: 'Jesus Christ, Son of God, have mercy upon me!'

He will not be put off by the crowd. He will not be put off by his blindness. Bartimaeus wants Jesus to come to him. Jesus stops and calls the blind man. Even in his blindness Bartimaeus jumps up and moves towards Jesus and asks that he may receive his sight. Jesus replies, 'Your faith has saved you.' And immediately the blind man sees.

Ponder
Think over the words, 'I once was blind but now I see.' Do we let Jesus pass by in our lives? Do we let him sleep or do we have a faith relationship with him?

Promise
Promise that you will call upon him today many times and say 'Jesus Christ, Son of God, have mercy upon me a sinner'.

Pray
Pray now these very words saying them slowly to the ever-present Lord: 'Jesus Christ, Son of God, have mercy upon me a sinner'.

Let the words help you to form a loving relationship with him. Take your time over each word and let the richness of each word enrich you.

Pray
Pray to Christ our Saviour:

> Be you my pole star, heavenly guide,
> Be my sure light over the world wide.
> Be you the Captain close at my side
> From the free flowing to the ebb tide.

When the storms rage, winds increase,
Draw me Lord to your deep peace.
Be you the Captain close at my side
From the free flowing to the ebb tide.

If life will ebb or if it will flow
The risen Christ will with us go.
Be you the Captain close at my side
From the free flowing to the ebb tide.

(Adam, 1989)

Lord from this world's stormy sea
Give your hand for lifting me
Lord lift me from the darkest night
Lord lift me into the realm of light
Lord lift me from this body's pain
Lord lift me up and keep me sane
Lord lift me from the things I dread
Lord lift me from the living dead
Lord lift me from the place I lie
Lord lift me that I never die

(Adam, 1985)

In your mercy deliver us from all evil:
Protect us from all that would destroy us.
As you guided Noah over the waters of the
    flood, hear us:
As you rescued Jonah from the deep, deliver us;
As you stretched out your hand to the sinking
    Peter, help us.
As you lifted your loved ones out of hell,
    uplift us,
And at the last bring us to the safety of your
    kingdom.

Leaving All

It is hard to remember that the Celtic wanderers lived at a time when most people did not travel further than the nearest town and many did not even do that. Travel was a dangerous occupation and never entered into unadvisedly, lightly or wantonly. In the times of Brendan most people never left the safety and security of their tribal community. The community gave protection and purpose; the community was a defence against not only human foes but also the powers of evil. To leave the safety and security of one's homeland was to enter into dangerous areas and face the unpredictable. Community also gave a person meaning and a position; out in strange lands all these securities would disappear, the traveller would be homeless and nameless. However, the lighter one travelled the less one would be endangered from robbers: the less goods a person carried the more likely they would be able to travel safely. Possessions can so quickly restrict our journeying and keep us tied to one place and fixed habits. Possessions can endanger our freedom and even our life. Jesus warned his disciples that 'a person's life is not made up of the things that they possess'. We are far greater than the sum of all our possessions; the Bible recognizes there is nothing valuable enough to give in exchange for our soul.

I can remember the day I was to leave home and all its security. I would leave behind my job and its income, my friends and their support and companionship. I would give up the freedom to roam where I liked, to come and go as I pleased. Instead of nights out with my mates I would spend nights in prayer and silence. Instead of gaining possessions I would learn to call nothing my own. I was fearful, I was anxious, I was far from certain but I was also setting out on a great adventure. There was a strange feeling that this is what I was being called to do. Instead of having much free time I would be compelled to go to church many times each day. I would not be allowed to speak except in worship for more than 12 hours out of every 24. It all sounded very restrictive, it would appear my life was going to be much narrower than before. For a while I felt this was so and wondered why I endured it. Why had I given up my freedom? Whenever a bell rang I had to stop doing what I was doing and answer the call to prayer. How could someone narrow their life like this? I wondered if I was becoming like a Pavlovian dog in the way I responded to certain stimuli. Then slowly, it seemed very slowly, there was a change, not in my surroundings but in me. I was beginning to discover new depths in the things I was doing and new depths in myself. I was learning to live to the glory of God – I am still learning – and gaining glimpses of glory. Ordinary tasks were being transformed in the way that only love can transform them. I began to understand how Jacob could work for seven years for love and it would seem a day. I was discovering how to step out of time and into eternity. I was learning that in love nothing that you give up for the beloved is a sacrifice and all that you give away enriches you: I am still learning that is truly 'more blessed to give than receive'. But this is jumping ahead. Let us ask with the poem, 'Shall I say farewell to my beautiful land, placing myself under Christ's yoke?'

In a time when most people never travelled further

than the local market town and probably never journeyed more than 20 miles away from home in their life time, there was a group of people that were travelling all the known world and beyond. These individuals were leaving all for the love of God. They were given the same name as the wandering stars, the planets, they were called the *peregrinatio*, the wanderers or the pilgrims. Yet this journey was not born of restlessness but of purpose. They saw life as road to God, as journey into the deeper presence and into eternity. St Columbanus wrote:

> Let us concern ourselves with things divine, and as pilgrims ever sigh for and desire our homeland: for the end of the road is ever the object of travellers' hopes and desires, and thus, since we are travellers and pilgrims in the world, let us ever ponder on the end of the road, that is of our life, for the end of the roadway is our home . . . Let us not love the roadway rather than the homeland, lest we lose our eternal home: for we have such a home that we ought to love it. Therefore let this principle abide with us, that on the road we so live as travellers and pilgrims, as guests of the world.
>
> (Walker, 1970, p. 97)

Many of the Celtic saints sought to live this way, and to journey towards the Promised Land of God, and deeper into God. Of the Welsh saint, Brynach, it was said:

> By thinking nothing of the place of his birth, by forsaking his own land, he sought to find it; by living in exile he hoped to reach home.
>
> (Duckett, 1959, p. 25)

55

Columbanus or Brynach would have been happy with the hymn 'This world is not my home, I am only passing through'. Yet for all this feeling of mobility and being driven forward, there was also an inner peace and a singleness of purpose. This was the hearing of a call by the beloved and seeking him throughout their lives. The best of the monasteries did not encourage travel for the sake of travel or vagrants travelling from monastery to monastery. If a monk wanted to go on pilgrimage he had to obtain permission from his bishop: there was need to discern that the journey was the will of God. When a teacher in the monastery of Samthann of Clonberry wanted to go on a wander he was severely reprimanded.

A certain teacher named Tairchellach approached the virgin and said, 'I am minded to put aside study and to give myself to prayer.'

The saint replied, 'What shall maintain your mind against straying thoughts if you neglect spiritual studies?'

The teacher then said, 'I desire to go overseas on pilgrimage.'

Samthann answered, 'Were God to be found in going overseas, I would also get into ship and go. But since God is near to all who call upon him, there is no constraint upon us to seek him overseas. For from every land there is a way to the kingdom of heaven.'

Pilgrimage was not just travel because of a feeling of restlessness, not even just for a sense of adventure; it had to be to do the will of God, and so for the love of God. Pilgrimage is a moving from where we are so that we can move deeper into the presence of God. The detachment from things is in order to attach ourselves closer to the Almighty. When asked, 'What makes a man or woman leave his father and mother?'

the Bible answers, 'Love'. The Celtic Christians had no doubt that those who left their homeland on pilgrimage did it for the love of God. If you looked at an outcrop of rock in the sea like Skellig St Michael off the Dingle Peninsula and thought that people sought to live there, you would decide immediately they must be either mad or lovers, disturbed in mind or disturbed by God. These were not restless wanderers but men and women who were in love with their God and were seeking out the best place to serve the beloved. St Patrick is the first to call himself a 'pilgrim for the love of God' and he used the word *peregrinatio*. It was not just a leaving of the native land; it was a leaving behind of all securities and one's old habits: the inner journey was often as difficult and as hazardous as the outward journey. In one way, the outward journey is meant to set in motion or deepen the inward journey; by letting loose of the past we can make a new start. The inner journey is not about intellectual knowledge but a knowing with the heart; it is a desire and longing to draw closer to God. The Shaker hymn that was often sung in the Appalachian mountains expresses this detachment for a purpose:

It's a gift to be simple,
It's a gift to be free,
It's a gift to come down where we ought to be,
And when we see ourselves in a way that's right,
We will live in a valley of love and delight.
(Foster, 1984, p. 69)

Whenever we move, we must give up something if we are to take on something new. Often we have to weigh up one against the other and decide which we want. In the story of the rich young ruler it would seem he had

57

everything the world admires. He had great possessions, he had youth and he was a person of authority. Yet he was aware that there was something lacking in his life. He came to Jesus with the question, 'What good deed must I do to possess eternal life?' On talking to him Jesus saw that this was a good-living young man who had much to offer. Jesus decided to invite him to be one of his followers and asked to him sell all that he had saying, 'Come, follow me.' At this moment there follows one of those great lines of the Bible: 'He went away sorrowful; for he had great possessions' (AV). He ought to have been delighted to have so much but it had become the master of him; he was possessed by his possessions. Because he could not let go of the things he had, he turned away from Jesus. There is a wonderful painting I once saw of a man with his back to Jesus; the man is hunched and walking into blackness: it is a painting of the rich young man unfulfilled going away into darkness. The question is, What do we love the most? There is no sacrifice too great for our beloved. If money has become our chief desire, and the increase of riches our first love, then we will not let anything stop us in our pursuit of the glitter and the gold.

The Celtic hermits and pilgrims often left everything in their journey into God, yet in leaving something all things became enriched. In giving up for their beloved Lord, their lives took on a new richness and glory. A world with love and adoration is always of much greater value than worldly wealth or position. There is a poem about the seventh-century hermit Marvan who is questioned by his brother Guare the King of Connaught, who looks at reasons for his becoming a hermit. It is to teach us where true peace and value lies.

Guare	Now Marvan, hermit of the grot,
	Why sleep'st thou not on quilted
	feathers? . . .
Marvan	I have a sheiling in the wood,
	None save my god has knowledge of it,
	An Ash-tree and a hazelnut
	Its two sides shut, great oak boughs roof it.

Marvan goes on to describe the freedom that it gives him and the beauty and peace that is all around him, and ends:

> Content I am my Saviour's good
> Should on this wood set my choice.
>
> Without one hour of war or strife
> Through all my life at peace I fare:
> Where better can I keep my tryst
> With our Lord Christ, O brother Guare.

For a moment the King of Connaught sees there is another way of living and it offers its own riches. The poem ends with Guare admitting:

> My glorious Kingship, yea! and all
> My Sire's estates that fall to me,
> My Marvan I would gladly give,
> So might I live my life with thee.
>
> (Graves, 1917, pp. 35–8)

The moving out and leaving of possessions is linked with vision and discovery. Are we willing to give up all that we have for the great treasure that we have discovered, a treasure that lay hidden beneath our feet for so long? Sadly many will go through life without ever discovering what is offered to them. It is not that God does not call or reveal himself, it is rather that we have ceased to see or hear; we have closed ourselves up to the mystery and the beauty that is about us and within us. When this happens we need again to travel, to move away from where we are and to give up habits that bind us. It is interesting to note how a great many of the Celtic pilgrims began the special journey late in their lives. In the case of Brendan this last journey of seven years was at the final stage of his life on earth. Columbanus left Ireland at a time when he was of some repute and in a position of great authority. Columbanus writes:

The man to whom little is not enough will not bene-fit from more . . . Love your person rather than your property, your soul more than your wealth: for it is yourself only and not your wealth that is wretched, and you should love yourself more than another's goods. For what is your own, except your soul? Then do not lose your one possession for the sake of naught. Have no mercy on transitory things, lest you lose what is eternal.

(Walker, p. 79)

Yet Columbanus and Brendan would leave their homeland only because they had a vision of a more wonderful land. Too often we cling only to what we can see now and fail to discover the treasure that is offered to us. I once read a story of a farmer in what was the Orange Free State. His land was hard to work due to lack of water. For years he laboured to no avail, crops failed and harvests were poor. In the end he sold the farm for a very small amount of money. The peo-ple who bought it had vision and believed that there was water to be found under the ground. They spent their money sinking wells and discovered a great underground lake. Soon the farm was prosperous indeed. The other poor man had been sitting on this great resource and did not know it. Too often we talk of God but do not realize the great love and power that is being offered. Too often we talk about God when we could be talking to him. We need to make space in our days for our God, and sometimes this means moving out from where we stand at the present. We must not leave it too late, let us heed the words of St Augustine of Hippo:

I was slow to love you, Lord,
your age-old beauty is still as new to me:
I was slow to love you!
You were within me,
yet I stayed outside
seeking you there;
in my ugliness I grabbed at
the beautiful things of your creation.
Already you were with me,
but I was still far from you.
The things of this world kept me away:
    I did not know then
that if they had not existed through you
they would not have existed at all.
Then you called me
and your cry overcame my deafness;
you shone out
and your light overcame my blindness;
you surrounded me with your fragrance
and I breathed it in,
so that now I yearn for more of you;
I tasted you

and now I am hungry and thirsty for you;
you touched me,
and now I burn with longing for your peace.
(Augustine of Hippo)
(Boldoni, 1987, p. 19)

Sometimes possessions come between not only us and
our God but they come between us and other people;
what we have can separate us from others. On Lindisfarne, St Aidan constantly gave away any money that
was given to him or he used the money to buy slaves
and then set them free. When Aidan was given a horse
by the king it was not long before he had given it away
to a beggar. Aidan preferred to walk and meet people
on their level; to ride a horse set him above the major-
ity of people he met, so he gave the horse away. Bede
tells us that when Colman left the monastery on
Lindisfarne in 664 the monastery had no possessions,
only a few cattle. The Lindisfarne monks were content
to live as poor brothers. Later, Cuthbert would leave
Lindisfarne for his own desert in the ocean, and he
chose to spend the last days of his life on the little
island of Inner Farne. He wanted to give up all to be
alone with his God. Time and again we hear of Celtic
monks leaving all to follow God: men and women
leaving the transient behind in exchange for the eternal.
Obviously, such an exchange is not so much a losing
as a finding, not so much a giving up as a taking on;
in the end this is an expression of love and fulfilment.

In a world where so many people are unfulfilled,
there is a constant desire for more and more. This
need to have so many possessions only reflects our
inner poverty. A long time ago I learnt the glorious
freedom of calling nothing my own. In the House
Rule of the Society of the Sacred Mission at Kelham

in Nottinghamshire I was told, 'The fullness of sacrifice demands the sacrifice of all earthly goods. No brother may therefore claim anything as his own, either for possession or enjoyment . . . no one should have anything that he cannot willingly lay aside.' This was a wonderful lesson to learn, for a life is so enriched when it is not measured by what one owns. It also means one can travel lightly and not be hampered by things. There is also a movement away from trust in possessions and material power to putting one's faith in God and in his might. In the end no possessions can save a person, and one day we will all be called to leave all behind. The more possessions we have the harder it is to leave them.

One of the hardest things to give up is responsibility. So often people say, 'I would like to help but I have responsibilities.' Perhaps it was because they had so many responsibilities that people like Brendan knew it was time to leave them and to move on to a new freedom. We must make sure we are not captives to systems and organizations in a way that prevents us from truly meeting and serving our God. Ideally we should be able to serve God through our daily work but there are times when it becomes necessary to separate ourselves from our normal routine and to give our attention fully to our God. At all times it is necessary to make sure that God is not edged out of our life by perpetual busyness. We need to create a system that calls us to make space in our days and to make room for God. To have a fixed time and fixed place for our prayers can prove very useful, especially if we have a good back-up system for when the first system fails. We need regularly to check out our relationship with our God and to make sure God is still given priority. It is amazing how we will let trivial events and unimportant commitments keep us from giving ourselves in love to our God. If we say we do not have the time to spend in prayer and meditation, we are saying that God is not very high on our agenda. Many of our troubles arise because we do not spend enough time with him who is our peace. The old evangelical hymn states it well:

> O what peace we often forfeit,
> O what needless pain we bear –
> All because we do not carry
> Everything to God in prayer!
> (Joseph Meddicott Scriven 1819–86)
> (*Mission Praise*, 1995)

More than that, surely if we truly love God we will want to spend as much time as possible rejoicing in his presence and love.

EXERCISES

PRAY

Pray carefully (or sing) the Irish eighth-century hymn:

> Be thou my vision, O Lord of my heart,
> be all else but naught to me, save that thou art:
> be thou my best thought in the day and the night,
> both waking and sleeping, thy presence my light.

> Be thou my wisdom, be thou my true word,
> be thou ever with me, and I with thee, Lord:
> be thou my great Father and I thy true son:
> be thou in me dwelling, and I with thee one.

Be thou my breastplate, my sword for the fight;
be thou my whole armour, be thou my
   true might;
be thou my soul's shelter, be thou my strong
   tower:
O raise thou me heavenward, great Power of
   my power.

Riches I heed not, nor man's empty praise:
be thou mine inheritance now and always;
be thou and thou only the first in my heart:
O Sovereign of heaven, my treasure thou art.

High King of heaven, thou heaven's bright Sun,
O grant me its joys after victory is won:
great Heart of my own heart, whatever befall,
be still thou my vision, O Ruler of all.

                              (Irish hymn, eighth century)

READ

Read the parable of the sower and see what prevents
the growth of the word of God. Mark 4.1–9.

PAUSE

Pause and let the Word of God get into your life. Make
room. Make a space in your day. Be still in the presence of God, let the awareness of the presence enter
deeply into your whole being. God seeks you out and
wants his love to grow in you. Be still and let God's
love have room to enter and grow.

PICTURE

Picture the sower. The seed is good seed and he scat-
ters it liberally everywhere. There is an openness and
a hopefulness in the sowing. Now carefully watch

growth and see what happens. The first seeds did not even get into the ground, it was too hard. Trodden by habit, the footpath was a place of movement and too hard for growth. At least the seed fed the birds; people might not benefit but God's creation does. Look at the rocky soil, it is very shallow yet it allows for growth. In fact seeds sown here seem to be the first to get going but had no real root and in the heat of the day they perished, having no staying power at all. See the seed that fell among weeds; it grew well, it showed promise but it was choked by what was around it. I am always amazed at the appearance of weeds and how they thrive. Thank God for the seed that grew and produced a good crop.

PONDER

There is nothing wrong with the generosity of the sower. There is nothing wrong with the seed. The fault lies in the soil. It is time for a little soil analysis. First it is necessary to recognize that in our lives we have all these different areas, as does the soil. We can so often be so busy that God cannot get near: he wants to speak to us, to come to us, but our habits and actions prevent him. Then there is so much that is shallow in all our lives; we lack depth, we skate the surface. We say we believe but we do not let those beliefs reach deep down in our lives; we live like non-believers, we do not show the fruits of God's love and generosity to us. There is no doubt we all have plenty of weeds to dig out – and remember weeds are virulent and will reappear. Too often all our good intentions are lost to distractions and things of lesser importance. Thank God that most of life is still fruitful and give thanks for the areas of growth and beauty.

PROMISE

Promise to let the love of God get into your life, to get into the depths of your being. Let nothing separate you from the love of God in Christ Jesus. Do not let God get crowded out of your day. Let the awareness of His love and presence grow in you.

PRAY

Lord open my life to your presence.
Come fill me with your peace,
Fill my days with your glory,
Fill my heart with your love,
That my life may overflow with your goodness
and bring forth the fruits of love and joy and peace.

PRAY

Lord of all power, I give you my will,
in joyful obedience your tasks to fulfil
Your bondage is freedom, your service is song,
and, held in your keeping, my weakness is strong.

(Jack C. Winslow)
(*Hymns Ancient and Modern Revised,* 1983)

Alone on a Stormy Sea

If you live on the Atlantic seaboard, you cannot ignore the sea; you will either love it or hate it. Whatever your feelings towards it you will respect its power and be amazed by its moods and perhaps its mystery. Anyone with a sense of adventure is attracted by the ocean. The love of sea is expressed in a poem attributed to St Columba:

> Beloved are Durrow and Derry,
> Beloved is pure Raphoe,
> Beloved is Drumhome the fruitful
> Beloved are Sords and Kells:
> But sweeter and lovelier far,
> The salt sea where the sea-gulls fly.
>
> (Columba)

Brendan, having been brought up in Kerry, must have learnt to sail at a very early age. He would learn how to navigate and how to respect the sea in all its powers. The curragh that he would learn to sail in was essentially the same boat as had been used for centuries. The same skin crafts would have been used on the east coast of Ireland to invade what is now England and Scotland, in fact people from Ireland colonized the west coast of Scotland and named the area Dalriada after their own homeland. Raiders from Ireland would have taken Patrick prisoner and sailed him away in such a curragh. It was in a curragh that Columba left Ireland and landed on Iona at 'Port a Curraich', the

Bay of the Curragh. These relatively small vessels were thoroughly tested as sea-going boats.

The building of a curragh is described at the beginning of the 'Voyage of Brendan':

> Brendan and his companions made a coracle, using iron tools. The ribs and frame were made of wood, as is the custom in those parts, and the covering was tanned ox-hide stretched over oak bark. They greased all the seams on the outer surface of the skin with fat and stored away spare skins inside the coracle, together with forty days' supplies, fat for waterproofing the skins, tools and utensils. A mast, a sail, and various pieces of equipment for steering were fitted into the vessel: then Brendan commanded his brethren in the name of the Father, Son and Holy Spirit to go aboard.
>
> (Webb, 1983, p. 214)

This small vessel would be their home and their church for a long sea voyage. There would be no room for luxuries or for privacy, these men would travel lightly and put their trust in God.

After longer journeys, sailors would have experiences to tell of when they returned to port. They would talk of storms and monsters, sometimes of mysterious islands and strange peoples. As always the western sea attracted the adventurer for there was the great unknown, unexplored territory that would test the bravest of men. Some would say the world ended here and no one could venture further. The west of Ireland was known as the edge of the world, beyond that was the great deep. In a strange way the deep of the ocean called to the deep in some people's lives and they felt

70

compelled to adventure. Like John Masefield's description in his poem 'Sea Fever':

> I must go down to the seas again, for the call
>   of the running tide
> Is a wild call and a clear call that may not be
>   denied;
> And all I ask is a windy day with the white
>   clouds flying,
> And the flung spray and the blown spume, and
>   the sea-gulls crying.
>
> I must go down to the seas again, to the vagrant
>   gypsy life,
> To the gull's way and the whale's way where the
>   wind's like a whetted knife;
> And all I ask is a merry yarn from a laughing
>   fellow-rover,
> And a quiet sleep and a sweet dream when the
>   long trick's over.
>
> (Masefield, 1936)

For Brendan there was something, or Someone, calling out there and it was not just the sea. Brendan was born into a group of sailing peoples, he would hear of legendary islands that appeared and disappeared on the horizon, such as the island of Hy Brazil which only appeared on rare occasions. He would experience the loss of crews and boats and know that the sea was mightier than anyone. No doubt he took part in boat blessings like this one from the Outer Hebrides:

> Before embarking on a journey, the voyagers stood round their boat and prayed to the God of the elements for a peaceful voyage over the stormy sea. The steersmen led the appeal, while the swish of the

waves below, the sough of the sea beyond, and the sound of the wind around blended with the voices of the suppliants and lent dignity and solemnity to the scene.

Helmsman	Be the ship blest
Crew	By God the Father blest
Helmsman	Be the ship blest
Crew	And by God the Son blest
Helmsman	Be the ship blest
Crew	By God the Spirit blest

All
God the Father,
And God the Son,
God the Spirit,
Blessing give,
Be the ship blest

Helmsman	What can afear With God the Father near?
Crew	Naught can we fear.
Helmsman	What can afear And God the Son is near?
Crew	Naught can we fear.
Helmsman	What can afear And God the Spirit near?
Crew	Naught can we fear.
All	God the Father, And God the Son, God the Spirit, Be with us here And ever near.

Helmsman
What care is bred
Being of all o'erhead?

Crew	No care is bred.
Helmsman	What care is bred
	The King of all o'erhead?
Crew	No care is bred.
Helmsman	What care is bred
	Spirit of all o'erhead?
Crew	No care is bred.
All	Being of all,
	The King of all,
	Spirit of all,
	Over our head
	Eternal fall,
	Near us sure
	For evermore.

(McLean, 1961, pp. 367–8)

Among his own private prayers Brendan could have uttered to God such a prayer as comes from the *Adiuator Laborantium*:

O helper of workers,
ruler of all good,
guard on the ramparts
and defender of the faithful,
who lift up the lowly
and crush the proud,
ruler of the faithful,
enemy of the impenitent,
judge of all judges,
who punish those who err,
Pure life of the living,
light and Father of lights,
shining with great light,
denying to none of the hopeful

73

your strength and help,
I beg that me, a little man
trembling and most wretched,
rowing through the infinite storm of this age,
Christ may draw after Him to the lofty
most beautiful haven of life.

(Clancy and Markus, 1994, p. 111)

Strong men, who knew the dangers and knowing they
might not return, said they would go out and not be
afraid for their God was with them. No doubt they
often recited the psalm:

If the Lord had not been on our side . . .
the waters would have closed over us,
the torrents have swept us away,
either would have drowned us
in their turbulent waves.
Blessed be the Lord who did not let us fall.

(Psalm 124)

These men were the ones who 'Went down to the sea
in ships . . . who had seen his wonders in the deep'.
These men had to be alert and responsive to their
environment or the sea would swallow them up. Such
journeying made these men what they were and gave
them a respect for mighty powers. They would face
loneliness and solitude, silence and storm; most of the
time there would be none near to help them except
their God. They would know the experience of the
Ancient Mariner:

Alone, alone, all, all alone,
Alone on a wide, wide sea!

And never a saint took pity on
My soul in agony . . .

I looked to heaven, and tried to pray;
But or ever a prayer had gusht,
A wicked whisper came, and made
My heart as dry as dust.

('Ancient Mariner', Part IV,
Samuel Taylor Coleridge)

This was no easy life. Time and again boats would go
out and not return. Women would wait anxiously in
storms and look out from headlands for the safe return
of their menfolk, those in monasteries would look out
for their brethren. Storms could drive boats miles off
course and it would take sailors a long time to return to
their homes. Sometimes they would return after being
given up as lost. This was a demanding way of life and
was for heroes and adventurers, not for the faint-hearted.

And now the Storm-blast came, and he
Was tyrannous and strong:
He struck with his o'ertaking wings,
And chased us south along.

With sloping mast and dipping prow . . .
The ship drove fast, loud roared the blast,
And southward aye we fled.

And now there came both mist and snow,
And it grew wondrous cold:
And ice, mast-high, came floating by,
As green as emerald.

('Ancient Mariner', Part I,
Samuel Taylor Coleridge)

Brendan's journey was in the northern hemisphere, not the southern, and he describes his encounters with icebergs:

> One day, when the masses were over, they noticed a column rising out of the sea. It seemed quite near at hand but turned out to be a good three days' journey away. When they reached it, Brendan gazed upwards but hardly could see the top because of its great height: it was higher than the sky. This column was covered with a most unusual canopy – so strange indeed that the coracle could pass through the opening in it but no one could tell of what substance it was made. It was the colour of silver and seemed harder than marble. The column was pure crystal.
>
> 'Ship the oars!' Brendan commanded. 'Take down the sails and hold back the ribs of the canopy.' The canopy was so big that it extended a mile on either side of the column and went down into the sea. 'Now draw the boat through the opening,' Brendan continued, 'and let us inspect the wonders of God our Maker.'
>
> (Webb, 1983, p. 236)

They would often say Psalms 27 and 29 in their daily services which they maintained in their curragh and these words would be familiar to them:

> Pay tribute to the Lord, you sons of God,
> tribute to the Lord of glory and power . . .
> The voice of the Lord over the waters!
> The Lord over the multitudinous waters!
> The voice of the Lord in power
> The voice of the Lord in splendour! . . .
> (Psalm 29.1–4)

For he shelters me under his awning
in times of trouble.

(Psalm 27.5)

God whose power is over the waters would be prayed
to for strength, for protection and for deliverance.
There would be many times on a long voyage when all
strength was gone and their only hope was in the love
and compassion of God. This is as true for us in our
journey through life. If we are adventuring and
extending ourselves there will be times when we have
been overstretched, times when we run out of energy,
times when we have no power of ourselves to help
ourselves. We will need to trust in God who is a very
present help in trouble: put our faith in the Almighty
who will not leave us nor forsake us. The fishermen of
the Hebrides have no illusions about the mightiness
and dangers of the sea. They would commit their
journey and themselves to God with such words as:

God the Father all-powerful all benign,
Jesu the Son of tears and of sorrow,
With Thy co-assistance, O Holy Spirit

The Three One, ever-living, ever-mighty,
    everlasting
Who brought the Children of Israel through
    the Red Sea,
And Jonah to land from the belly of the
    great creature of the ocean,

Who brought Paul and his companions in
    the ship,
From the torment of the sea, from the dolour
    of the waves,

From the gale that was great, from the storm
   that was heavy.
. . . Sain us and shield and sanctify us,
Be Thou, King of the elements seated at
   our helm,
And lead us in peace to the end of our journey.

With winds, mild, kindly, benign, pleasant,
Without swirl, without whirl, without eddy,
That would do no harmful deed to us.
We ask all things of Thee, O God,
According to Thine own will and word.

(Carmichael, 1983, p. 329)

The sea was not romanticized. It always held a danger
in its wildness. This was an element that humans could
co-operate with, but they could not control it. Beccan
says Columba:

> crossed the wave-strewn wild region, foam-flecked,
> seal-filled, savage, bounding, seething, white-
> tipped . . . In the Trinity's care he sought a ship –
> good his leaving – on high with God, who always
> watched him morning and evening.

(Clancy and Markus, 1994, pp. 146–7)

We need to be made aware of our frailty in this world,
for then we know where we stand and that is a
strength. The psalmist says, 'It is good for me that I
have suffered.' We need to know that we are not invin-
cible and at all times we are dependent on the mercy
of our God. To voyage on the sea in an open boat will
remind us of this at any time. No wonder there are
many prayers that are sea-related. Here are another
two prayers from the Hebrides:

Thou Being who Jonah didst safely land
Out from the bag of the sow of the sea,
Bring thou myself to beckoning strand
With lading and ship entrusted to me.

(McLean, 1961, p. 369)

O Thou who dost dwell in the soaring sky,
On us the tide-mark of glad blessing lie,
Carry us over the crest of the seas,
Carry us to a haven of peace,
Our shipmen bless and our ship fore and aft,
Our anchors bless and the blades of our craft,
Each stay, each halyard, each voyaging man,
Keep our tall stepped masts with their mainsails'
    span,
O King of the elements, strong and taut,
That with good success we homeward make port:
My self sitting down in the helmsman's seat,
It is God's own Son sets my course complete.

(McLean, 1961, p. 376)

As far as Brendan was concerned there was no other
way to the Promised Land of the saints than across the
sea roads. He was well aware of all the dangers and the
hardships that he would have to face. He knew that
they might never return to Ireland, but having heard
the call he went out in faith. Though he did not know
what lay ahead, he had a strong belief that his God
would not leave him or forsake him. He knew that in
his adventuring he would learn more of the power and
the love of God. If we are afraid to venture we will
never enter into the fullness of life. If we are afraid of
death we will never live life to the full. If we avoid the
deep things of the world we will not be able to talk of
the depth of the mystery and wonder of God. If we

have never run out of strength or energy, if we have never come to the end of our own resources and ability to cope, we do not know what we are talking about when we talk of a Saviour. Brendan perhaps knew the words of St Irenaeus in his writing 'Against Heresies': 'The glory of God is a man or a woman who is fully alive.' If we are to know much of the great depths of God we have to learn to live in the deep. The call of God is to adventurous living, to extend our vision and ourselves. If we are only fair weather Christians we will never experience his wonders in the deep or the depth of his wonder.

EXERCISES

READ

Read Romans 8.35–39. Affirm that 'Nothing can separate us from the love of God in Christ Jesus.' Strengthen that affirmation with the words following:

> In heavenly love abiding,
> no change my heart shall fear:
> and safe is such confiding,
> for nothing changes here.
> The storms may rage about me,
> my heart may low be laid,
> but God is round about me,
> and can I be dismayed?
>
> Wherever He may guide me,
> no want shall turn me back:
> my Shepherd is beside me,
> and nothing can I lack.
> His wisdom ever waketh,
> His sight is never dim,

He knows the way He taketh,
and I will walk with Him.

Green pastures are before me,
which yet I have not seen;
bright skies will soon be o'er me,
where the dark clouds have been.
My hope I cannot measure,
my path to life is free,
my Saviour has my treasure,
and He will walk with me.

(Anna Laetitia Waring 1823–1910)

PONDER

Think over these words from Columbanus:

> Seek no further concerning God: those who wish to
> know the great deep must first review the natural
> world. For knowledge of the Trinity is properly
> likened to the depths of the sea, according to that
> saying of the Sage. And the great depth who can
> find it out? If then man wishes to know the deepest
> ocean of divine understanding, let him first if he
> is able scan that visible sea, and the less he finds
> himself to understand of those creatures which lurk
> beneath the waves, the more let him realize that he
> can know less of the depths of its Creator: and as
> he ought and should let him venture to treat less of
> Creator than of creature since none can be compe-
> tent in the greater if he has not explored the less,
> and when a man is not trusted in the lesser, in the
> greater how should he be trusted? For why, I ask,
> does a man ignorant of earthly things examine the
> heavenly?

(Walker, p. 89)

PONDER

Take to heart the prayer St Teresa of Avila had as her bookmark:

> Trust in God
> Let nothing disturb you,
> Let nothing frighten you;
> All things pass:
> God never changes.
> Patience achieves
> all it strives for.
> He who has God
> finds he lacks nothing.
> God alone suffices.

(Teresa of Avila 1515–82)

Awakening the Christ

More than once I have offered people a cheque for £10,000. I am so generous! There is only one condition attached to the gift; it is that they frame it and do not cash it. They can put it in their homes and tell people how generous I am, they can even talk about what they would do with the money, as long as they leave the cheque alone and keep it just on display. I tell you this, for this is my experience of the faith of many people. They say that God has given them great riches, they talk of his peace and his love, but they do not seem to benefit from them. So often people talk of the power of God but seem to ignore that power in their lives. Sometimes people have to come to the end of their own resources before they discover how generous and powerful is their God. It is often when our own might fails that we discover how mighty is our God.

The sea is a place where you soon discover your own smallness and the mighty greatness of the elements that are around you. Time and again Brendan and his crew were brought to the limits of their own abilities. They could do no more and had to let go and put their trust in God. It is important to know that they had done their bit, they had used their powers and abilities, they were beyond their own resources and needed a Saviour.

One day they sighted an island close at hand, but when they were approaching the shore, a breeze

85

blew them back out to sea away from the harbour.
Round and round the island they sailed for four
days without being able to find anywhere to land.
The monks, with tears in their eyes, implored the
Lord to come to their aid, for they had come to the
end of their strength and were completely exhausted.
After three days of fasting and unceasing prayer,
they came upon a small inlet so narrow that only
one boat could enter.

(Webb, 1983)

There is no doubt that Brendan and his crew felt that
God always guided them in the deep. These sailors
knew that to survive on stormy seas and in strange
waters you needed a good helmsman and so they
called upon their God. The psalms, familiar through
daily recitation, gave the sailors images of hope and
trust and reminded them that God is in control. They
would regularly say aloud Psalm 124.1–6:

If the Lord had not been on our side . . . the waters
would have closed over us, the torrent would have
swept us away, either would have drowned us in
their turbulent waves. Blessed be the Lord who did
not let us fall.

They would recite Psalm 107 which says that God is
good and his love is everlasting'. Verses 23–32
expressed how they often must have felt:

Others, taking ships and going to sea,
were plying their business across the ocean;
they too saw what the Lord could do,
what marvels in the deep!

He spoke and raised a gale,
lashing up towering waves.
Flung to the sky, then plunged to the depths,
they lost their nerve in the ordeal,
staggering and reeling like drunkards
with all their seamanship adrift.

Then they called to the Lord in their troubles
and he rescued them from their sufferings,
reducing the storm to a whisper
until the waves grew quiet,
bringing them, glad at the calm,
safe to the port they were bound for.

Let these thank the Lord for his love,
for his marvels on behalf of men.

(Psalm 107.23–32)

We must remember it is likely that the voyagers with
Brendan did not carry a book of the psalms with them
or even a Gospel book, they carried them in their
hearts. Through daily recitation they knew all of the
150 psalms and continued to recite them throughout
their journey. As the curragh was their home and their
church, many of the psalms must have taken on a
special meaning while they were on the sea. The
psalms were learnt in worship; that is not just through
recitation but through devotion. They were learnt as
they directed them in love to their God, so they were
full of meaning and gave them hope. Regularly they
would say, and in saying it find hope: 'The Lord is
my strength, my shield, my heart puts its trust in
him' (Psalm 28.7). When the storms were beyond
human strength, they put themselves under the

helmsman who was stronger than they were, and that helmsman was the Christ.

> God of the elements, glory to thee
> For the lantern-guide of the ocean wide;
> On my rudder's helm may thine own hand be,
> and thy love abaft on the heaving sea.
>
> (McLean, 1961, p. 371)

As a guide and a pilot through life and its storms they learnt to call upon their Lord:

> O Christ will you help me on the wild waves?
> A dear pure pilgrimage
> subduing faults, a body chaste,
> a life of poverty, lowly and secluded
> occur often to my mind.
>
> The gift of piety, the gift of pilgrimage,
> the gift of repentance for my soul,
> O Christ without reproach
> grant them all to me.
>
> (Irish, tenth century)

No doubt one of the Scripture passages that often came to mind was the stilling of the storm (Matthew 8.23–34). Once again it would seem that all started well; either the disciples are rowing or letting a gentle wind carry them along. Jesus has used the sea to get away from the crowds, he is tired and asleep in the stern of the boat. Suddenly the craft is struck by a storm, a mighty wind comes rushing from the hills; the waves rise and the wind continues to increase. Even the fishermen become afraid. They bale out, they struggle with the rudder, they wrestle with the sails; they do everything they can but to no avail. It looks as if the little craft will sink. All this while Jesus sleeps. Now they awaken him and call, 'Lord, save us for we are perishing!' Jesus awakens, stands up and speaks to the wind and the waves and they become calm. Danger passes and the disciples also become calm, that is, until they land among the tombs and have to face the madman of Gadara.

Here is a man whose mind is as stormy as the wild sea and as restless as the waves. The disciples again are afraid of being overwhelmed. Jesus is still in control and he brings calm to the madman and a new peace to the disciples. The disciples ask, 'Who is this that the wind and the waves obey him?' They know the answer can be only God: it is God who stills the waves and the madness of the peoples.

The other thing to notice in this event is that Jesus remains in the back of the boat and asleep until he is called upon. The disciples did all they could but they needed a power beyond their power. It is not that Jesus is a last resort; rather his power comes into play only when we have extended ourselves and stretched our abilities. We learn time and again God will not do for us what we can do for ourselves. However, the danger for many is that they let Jesus sleep, they never call upon him or trust in his mighty power. It would seem that many Christians of today do not know the living Lord except as a sleeping partner. They talk about him, they theorize about him, they hold meetings about him but they do not talk to him. Too many people are unaware of the presence and power of their God. This is not so with Brendan. Time and again after working to the uttermost he knows it is time to call on the Almighty:

God is our helper. He is our captain and guide and will steer us out of danger. Just leave the sails and let Him do as He will with his servants in their boat.

(Webb, 1983, p. 215)

Again Brendan advises:

You will tire yourselves out. Is not the Lord our helmsman? Then leave it to him and he will direct us where he wills.

(Webb, 1983, p. 228)

When the curragh was in an area where the water was clear, the crew saw that they were surrounded by all sorts of sea creatures. They were so afraid that they asked Brendan to pray quietly lest he disturb the sea creatures and they would then be attacked by them.

Brendan chaffed them: I am surprised at your foolishness. What – are you afraid of these creatures? Have you not several times landed on the monarch of the deep, the beast who eats all other sea creatures? Why, you have sat down on his back and sung psalms, have even gathered sticks, lighted a fire and cooked food – and all this without showing fear. Then how can you be afraid of these? Is not our Lord Jesus Christ the Lord of Creation? Can he not make all creatures docile?

(Webb, 1983, p. 236)

To illustrate he meant what he said, Brendan then sang at the top of his voice. The fish rose and swam round and round the boat but did not come too close to it. No doubt Brendan would have been happy to use the prayer that is attributed to St Columba:

Alone with none but thee, my God,
I journey on my way:
What need I fear, when thou art near,
O King of night and day?
More safe I am within thy hand,
Than if a host did round me stand . . .

The child of God can fear no ill,
His chosen dread no foe;
We leave our fate with thee, and wait
Thy bidding when we go.
'Tis not from chance our comfort springs,
Thou art our trust, O King of kings.

(Ancient hymn author unknown
sometimes attributed to St Columba)

There is no doubt that if we are truly alive we all have our share of storms. There are times when we will be disturbed out of our security and complacency and called to launch out into the deep. Time and again we will be called to adventure and risk so that we remain fully alive and sensitive to our world, the people in it and to our God. The strange thing about our modern world is that easy travel seems to have helped to destroy a sense of adventure. Due to television showing us the world, and shops in the high street being much the same the world over, there is a feeling we have been there and seen it all. People seem to want be settled and secure rather than to adventure and launch into the depths of life. Still in every heart there is a longing for adventure, a feeling that we are being called to something or by Someone to what is far greater and better than what we have experienced. We know in our heart we are called to cross our own personal deserts and brave our own personal darkness and storms to come to the Promised Land; it is then we need know we are not alone and rejoice that our God is with us. Let us heed the call to extend ourselves, to adventure and to put our hand into the hand of God.

EXERCISES

PRAY

Pray, knowing that the Christ has called us long before we call upon Him:

You who called us to hope in your name,
which is the first of all creation,
open the eyes of our heart
that we may know you
who alone remains Highest among the highest
and Holiest among the holy.

Save those of us who are in affliction,
have mercy on the lonely,
raise up those that are fallen, be manifest to those
    that are in need,
heal the sick,
bring back those of your people that go astray.
Feed the hungry,
redeem the captives,
lift up those that are weak,
comfort the faint hearted.

(Clement of Rome, first century)

READ

Read again the stilling of the storm (Matthew 8.23–34). Realize that the awakening of the Christ in your life is not so much a movement on Christ's part as on your own. If anyone has to awaken it is you to the presence of the Lord who is ever watchful and awaits our calling on him.

> His wisdom ever waketh,
> His sight is never dim,
> He knows the way he taketh,
> and I will walk with him.

It is our own sleepiness and blindness that prevent us from seeing him; it is our own deafness and sensitivity that prevent us from hearing him. Awakening the Christ is to open ourselves to his presence, his power and his love. It is to become aware that he is in the same boat as we are, that he travels with us. Say to the ever-present Christ the words of the poem by Levi Yitzchak:

> Where I wander – You!
> Where I ponder – You!
> Only You, You again, always You!
> You! You! You!!
> When I am gladdened – You!
> When I am saddened – You!
> Only You, You again, always You!
> You! You! You above! You below!
> In every trend, at every end,
> Only You, You again, always You!
> You! You! You!!
>
> (Yitzchak, 1986)

It is not that we make the Christ wake or come to us; He is always there, ever present and waiting for us to turn and call upon him. Take some time affirming his presence and calling upon Him. Affirm:

Christ with me, Christ before me, Christ behind me,
Christ in me, Christ beneath me, Christ above me.
Christ on my right, Christ on my left,
Christ when I lie down, Christ when I sit down,
Christ when I arise,
Christ in the heart of everyone who thinks of me,
Christ in the mouth of everyone who speaks of me,
Christ in every eye that sees me,
Christ in every ear that hears me.

Learn that 'in him we live and move and have our being' and that the Lord is your light and your salvation.

The Place of Our Resurrection

There are many Celtic folk tales that have a similar sadness to the story of the return of Oisin. This splendid man had been drawn into the land beyond known as 'Tir-na-nOg', the Land of the Ever Young. In Tir-na-nOg time was without measure, ten or even a thousand days were like one day. If Oisin has remained there a hundred or a thousand years he would not have changed, he would have the same vigour and strength of limb as when he arrived. But a strange longing to return to his homeland entered his heart and influenced his relationship with Niamh of the Golden Hair. At last Niamh said to him, 'Go if you must and then come back to me refreshed.'

Oisin promised that he would return. It was hard to say how long he had been in this pleasant land, time passes quickly when you are enjoying yourself. It could have been well over 30 years since he first came and he looked the same as on the day he arrived. Now he was ready to leave on the same horse that brought him to the Otherworld.

'Remember, Oisin, remember not to dismount from your horse. It is from this world and carries this world with it. While you are on its back you belong to this world. Dismount it and you will immediately belong to the world from whence you came. Do not think your homeland will be the same as when you left it, the years will have brought about many changes.'

Oisin smiled at Niamh and nodded. As he rode away she wept for she knew he would not return.

Oisin came at a gallop into the world he left many years before, little did he know how long ago. Somehow the landscape had changed, it did not look so large, and many trees had gone; a fortress that he had known well was now a green mound with no signs of stones. A new broad road ran across what had been green fields. In the evening he came upon a group of children who were trying to lift a great standing stone which had fallen on one of them. On looking closer Oisin realized these were not children but full-grown adults. They were so puny they were hardly men at all. These little men told him how the race of heroes had gone like the wind and were no more. Oisin himself had passed into legend. Oisin turned his horse until he could grip the fallen stone. He tensed every muscle and heaved the great stone, sending it flying and freeing the trapped man. At the same moment, the saddle band snapped with the strain. Oisin began to fall to the earth. He grabbed for the reins but the horse shied away. As he toppled over, the horse disappeared. As he touched the ground, his skin wrinkled, his hair turned grey and much of it fell out, his bones became brittle and he became old. Soon Oisin would return to the dust from whence he came. For all his glimpse of the Land Beyond, for all his experience he was a man of the earth and to earth he would return.

The new faith, that Oisin was supposed to have heard from St Patrick, brought a new hope for weak and perishable humankind: the promise of the resurrection and eternal life. The Christians proclaimed the God who can make all things new. They put their trust in God who loved them and would not let them perish but offered them eternal life. Some of these Christians would be familiar with the prayers of St Augustine of Hippo, such prayers as:

Good and gracious God, to turn away from you
　is to fall
To turn to you is to rise
To abide with you is to remain forever.

(Augustine of Hippo)

In time the Celtic Christians talked of finding 'the place of their resurrection'. This was not somewhere after death but to be found in this world when they fulfilled their vocation; the place of their resurrection is the place where God's will is fulfilled. When God's will is done we enter into his kingdom, time is suspended and we enter into eternity by being at one with the Eternal God. When we come to the place of our resurrection we also know that we have come home, we have arisen and come to our Father. This resurrection is not a one-off event but happens to us time and time again. Time and again we will wander from God and from life, time and again we will fail to do his will and stand outside of his kingdom, and our God awaits our return. God waits to renew, refresh and restore us. Our God is a renewing God who makes all things new. The Risen Lord is able to renew each of us.

A woman on the island of Harris was afflicted with leprosy and became an outcast, her body dying more than living. She lived alone on the seashore, gathering shellfish to eat and plants from the dunes. In time all her flesh renewed itself and she became whole and wholesome once more. It is said that she wrote the following:

> It were as easy for Jesus
> To renew the withered tree
> As to wither the new
> Were it his will so to do.

> Jesu! Jesu! Jesu!
> Jesu! meet it were to praise him.
>
> (Carmichael, 1983, Vol 1, p. 39)

It is a pity that so many Christians talk as if the resurrection was some future event of which they have no experience. If we look at ourselves as human beings we discover that our bodies are dying and being renewed all the time. The resurrection of the body is not a one-off future event; it is something that happens to us every day, in fact at every single moment of our existence. Our bodies are made up of living cells that are changing every second of our life. Every one of us has something like sixty million million cells. Every single second of every minute of every hour, five million cells die, and another five million are born. Every minute three hundred million cells go through death and resurrection, every minute we are being reborn. Our bodies are in a continual state of death and resurrection. I find it so easy to say, 'I believe in the resurrection of the body.' It is a little harder to decide *which* body, as I have already had so many different bodies in growing from infant to full manhood. Yet, of each of the bodies recorded on photographs I can say, 'That's me and nobody else, and nobody else's body.' So much of God's creation goes through similar patterns of death and resurrection that it is beyond doubt that God can give us another body as it pleases him.

Not only is the resurrection of the body an ongoing and more-than-once event but we experience many other resurrections in our lives. We change and change again; old patterns, old relationships die and new ones are formed. We will only die fully if we cease to change. There is a suggestion in the Scripture that in fact we move from glory to glory. This is not to belittle the resurrection that we shall experience after death; it should rather enhance it for greater glories lie ahead. When the resurrection comes we will be able to say, 'You have kept the best until now.'

As the resurrection is an ongoing affair there are places that are beneficial to our rising and of course it follows there are places that can drag us down. There are also places where we do not experience anything and they are the most dangerous of all. At least as Christians if we die we know we will rise again. We are not afraid of death so we are able to live our lives fully. Those who fear death are afraid to live. Anyone who is afraid of death will not be able to adventure or move for fear. Our Lord came to free us from this fear and to give us the opportunity to enter into life and life which is eternal. We are given the opportunity to arise each day:

> New every morning is the love
> Our wakening and uprising prove:
> through sleep and darkness safely brought,
> restored to life and power and thought.

> (John Keble)
> (*Hymns Ancient and Modern*, 1983)

The ability to arise each day in the power of God is expressed in Kuno Myer's translation of 'The Deer's Cry' which is credited to St Patrick. Time and again we are to affirm, 'I arise today.'

> I arise today
> Through a mighty strength, the invocation of
>   the Trinity,
> Through belief in the threeness,

Through confession of the Oneness
Of the Creator of creation.

I arise today,
Through the strength of Christ's birth with
    his baptism,
Through the strength of his crucifixion with
    his burial,
Through the strength of his resurrection with
    his ascension,
Through the strength of his descent for the
    judgement of doom.

I arise today
Through the strength of the love of the
    cherubim,
In obedience of angels,
In the service of archangels,
In the hope of resurrection to meet with
    reward.
In the prayers of patriarchs,
In the prediction of prophets,
In the preaching of apostles,
In the faith of confessors,
In the innocence of holy virgins,
In the deeds of righteous men.

I arise today
Through the strength of heaven:
Light of sun,
Radiance of moon,
Splendour of fire,
Speed of lightning,
Swiftness of wind,
Depth of sea,

Stability of earth,
Firmness of rock.

I arise today,
Through God's strength to pilot me:
God's might to uphold me,
God's wisdom to guide me,
God's eye to look before me,
God's ear to hear me,
God's word to speak for me,
God's hand to guard me,
God's way to lie before me,
God's host to save me . . .

(Meyer, 1911, p. 25)

The Celtic Christians often looked for the place of their resurrection. There is no doubt it was the place that they expected to die in, but it was also the place that they hoped to live in and fulfil God's will in before they died. If death came quickly that did not matter as long as they had come to do his will. There is no need to fear death or the many deaths if you believe in him who has conquered death. This is embodied in many monastic rules. The Society of the Sacred Mission, with whom I trained, had in its Principles:

> If you have given your whole life to God, why should you prefer to lose it in this way rather than that? . . . If it cost you your life, what better could you ask than the time of trial be very short, since the reward is the same?

(Principles, 1951)

The resurrection is promised to those who do his will. When we fulfil what God has called us to do we come to the Promised Land, we share in eternity. Our vision of this may not be as clear as we would like it to be, but the facts are true. The sad comment on this is that many talk about it but few fully enter it; many want the adventure and the experience but are unwilling (and that is the right word) to pay the price. We need learn to live as we pray, 'Your kingdom come. Your will be done in us as it is in heaven.' Many stand peering into the distance when they are invited to step over into glory. R. S. Thomas has expressed this when he says:

> You can come in
> You can come a long way . . .
> But you won't be inside.
>> (Thomas, 1993)

There are others with eyes and hearts cleansed who not only behold but also enter eternity. Some discover nothing is too common to be raised. God comes in ordinary bread and wine, in ordinary people, in ordinary places. In fact the strange thing about the ordinary is if you look close enough, whatever it is, it is filled with the extra-ordinary. For much of our lives we walk as if in a fog, not seeing clearly, and unaware of the glory of our God. To live without recourse to God is to live a lie, for we could not exist without him. We are called to seek for him until we see and know him. When we come to the place of our resurrection we can say with Augustine:

> We shall rest and we shall see,
> We shall see and we shall know,
> We shall know and we shall love,
> We shall love and we shall praise.

Behold our end which is no end.
(Augustine of Hippo)
(Tutu, 1995)

We need to train ourselves in awareness to open our eyes to the Presence that is all about us. We need to walk with God in the way the Hebridean people walked with God. It is good to notice the expression of joy in this affirmation, and to find the same joy and express it in our prayers:

> The path I walk, Christ walks it. May the land in
> which I am be without sorrow.
> May the Trinity protect me wherever I stay, Father,
> Son and Holy Spirit.
> Bright angels walk with me – dear presence – in
> every dealing.
> In every dealing I pray then that no one's poison
> may reach me.
> The ninefold people of heaven of holy cloud, the
> tenth force of the stone earth.
> Favourable company, they come with me, so that
> the Lord may not be angry with me.
> May I arrive at every place, may I return home:
> may the way in which I spend be a way
> without loss.
> May every path before me be smooth, man woman
> and child welcome me.
> A truly good journey! Well does the fair Lord show
> us a course, a path.

(Davies and Bowie, 1995, p. 27)

This should give us the confidence to realize that we are on the path of God, not only on his path but in his Presence and his kingdom.

After journeying across the ocean and through the liturgy for seven years, Brendan and his crew were offered guidance to the Land of Promise by the steward of the Island of Birds where once again they had celebrated the feast of Pentecost. As they left, the last words they heard from the island were, 'May the God of our salvation grant you a safe journey!' After travelling for 40 days they were enveloped in a great darkness, so thick that they could hardly see each other. Once again we must realize that those who fear the darkness will never be able to venture far or come to the fulness of light. This darkness is like the cloud that hides the glory of God. It is a pity that so many people are put off by the cloud for it is often close to the glory. Brendan did not understand what the cloud was but moved forward in faith. Once they passed this dark cloud a brilliant light shone all around them and they came to the shore. At last they had come to the Land of Promise.

They were met by a young man who called each of them by their name and said, 'Blessed are they that dwell in thy house, O Lord. They shall praise your name for ever.' Brendan was also told that there is no darkness ever in this land for 'Christ himself is our light.' Little was said about this land for words of this world of ours cannot describe it but it was obviously a world of great beauty and wonder. It is difficult to return to the ordinary everyday world after such an experience but we so quickly do so. It took Brendan seven years, if not his whole life, to come to the Land of Promise yet suddenly there was a direct route back to Ireland and the monastery at Clonfert. He was told that he had not been allowed to find the Land of Promise immediately because the Lord Christ wished him to experience the wonders and richness of the deep first of all. It is our journey through this world, even its darkness, that prepares us for the wonders and delights of the world to come. God gives himself to us in this world, that we may seek him and enjoy him, until we come to him in the fullness of life eternal.

EXERCISES

PRAY

A prayer I often use comes from the Outer Hebrides and expresses well a situation we all experience: we believe in the Presence but we are faced with clouds and darkness; this darkness is a reality but so is the Presence of our God. Even when we do not feel the Presence we can still affirm it:

> Though the dawn breaks cheerless on this
> isle today,
> my spirit walks in a path of light.
> For I know my greatness.
> Thou hast built me a throne within thy heart.
> I dwell safely within the circle of thy care.
> I cannot for a moment fall out of the everlasting
> arms.
> I am on my way to glory.

(Maclean, 1937)

READ

Read 1 Corinthians 15.50–58. Look over your life and realize how many times you have already been changed. Take out your family photographs and see how many bodies you have already been given. Give thanks to God for each stage of life, each time you have risen to newness of life, each time you have passed through darkness to light. Know that whatever

107

has happened to you, you are still alive and God still loves you. He invites you to not to admit defeat, to seek to do his will and to work for his kingdom. Affirm in the love and Presence of God:

> All shall be Amen and Alleluia.
> We shall rest and we shall see,
> We shall see and we shall know,
> We shall know and we shall love,
> We shall love and we shall praise.
> Behold our end which is no end.

PRAY

Pray that you may be delivered from all that prevents you from adventuring:

> O Lord, we beseech thee to deliver us from the fear of an unknown future; from fear of failure; from fear of poverty; from fear of bereavement; from fear of loneliness; from fear of sickness and pain; from fear of age; from fear of death.
>
> Help us, O Father, by thy grace to love and fear thee only, fill our hearts with cheerful courage and loving trust in Thee: through our Lord and Master Jesus Christ.

(Tutu, 1995)

Homecoming

The difference between most Celtic pilgrims, who went out for the love of God, and ourselves is that they did not expect to return from their pilgrimage. When they set out to look for the Land of Promise or the place of their resurrection, once they had arrived, they aimed to stay. Often it was only circumstances or opposition from rulers that made the pilgrims for the love of God move on again, and usually it was further forward not back. For the Celtic pilgrim, on the road of life, there was no looking back. No one can return to where they have been, for all things move and change. Nostalgia for the past was not something the Celtic pilgrims suffered from; they had a greater desire to move towards the Land of Promise and to be fully at home in the present. These pilgrims saw themselves very much as guests in this world and on the road to God.

Let us concern ourselves with things divine, and as pilgrims ever sigh for and desire our homeland: for the end of the road is ever the object of travellers' hopes and desires, and thus, since we are travellers and pilgrims in the world, let us ever ponder on the end of the road, that is of our life, for the end of the roadway is our home . . . Let us not love the roadway rather than the homeland, lest we lose our eternal home: for we have such a home that we ought to love it. Therefore let this principle abide with us, that on the road we so live as travellers and pilgrims, as guests of the world.

(Walker, 1970, p. 97)

Columbanus left Bangor; like Abraham (Hebrews 11.8), who inspired him, he went out in faith not knowing where he was going but seeking the Land of Promise. More than once he would have to move on. The only time Columbanus thought of returning to Ireland, because of severe opposition, a storm prevented him and he took this as a sign to go forward not back. When Brendan left Clonfert in his curragh, he left behind all his securities and position not knowing whether he would return or not. Many had set out into the Atlantic before him and had not come back. Brendan knew that the sea could so easily swallow up him and his little crew. The Celtic pilgrim saw it was better to die in adventure than to remain fixed in a place where one was not fulfilled. In Brendan's case, if he had not returned, there would have been no story, no one to tell of the adventures on the high sea or the coming to the Land of Promise. In single-mindedness, Brendan set out to journey into God. It took seven years, if not his lifetime, and it is the build-up of those years and dedication that bring Brendan through the fog and into the Land of Promise.

One of the legends concerning Brendan tells of how he could not listen to earthly music because he had heard heavenly music. Whenever music was being played he blocked his ears with wool so that he would remember the heavenly music and not be distracted from it. He must have missed many wonderful tunes, yet at the same time he warns us not to be distracted from our journey into God. If we are to serve our God and seek his kingdom we will have to be single-minded.

There are many things that would distract us from reaching our homeland. Throughout our lives we need check what have become priorities to us and make sure we have not left our God for other attractions.

One of the stories of Jesus, told only in St Luke's Gospel, tells of a young man enticed away from his home and homeland by all that glitters. It is in Luke 15 that we hear of the prodigal son. One of the briefest descriptions I ever heard of this story was in three short sentences or scenes: 'Sick of home – homesick – home.' Someone once said to me, 'Home is where we are treated like royalty and act like fools.' It is amazing how we take our homes and our loved ones for granted, how we fail to appreciate what we have. The prodigal son, sick of home, wanders off into a far country and for a while enjoys himself doing all the sorts of things that youths get up to in their travels. One day he wakes up and realizes what he has lost, because now he has run out of money and friends. He finds himself alone in a tough world. This is a time of famine and he is living like an animal. This might be described as the desert time, not by choice but by accident. He begins to feel hunger and is ready to eat pigswill. In the depths of his dereliction he becomes aware of a yearning for his home, and the grace and generosity of his father. He says to himself, 'I will leave this place and go to my father and say: Father, I have sinned against heaven and against you; I no longer deserve to be called your son; treat me as one of your paid servants.' All this time the father has been waiting and longing for the return of his son. As the son journeys home, the father runs to meet him, clasps him in his arms and kisses him. The son says what he has rehearsed, he admits his unworthiness. The father is overjoyed at his return. The son does not get time to say, 'Treat me as one of your paid servants', for the father welcomes him home as a son and celebrates his return. The father enfolds him in his love and in his forgiveness; this is a time for rejoicing.

If only we would turn, our God is ready to welcome us and to enfold us. If we so choose, we can make every day a homecoming, every day we can take time and turn to our God. God has never left us; if we draw near to Him, He draws near to us. God is ever willing to welcome us with open arms. Often the Hebridean crofter would turn to God and allow himself to be enfolded by him; moments like this are homecomings and entering into the kingdom, times when we express that 'we dwell in him and he in us'.

God to enfold me,
God to surround me,
God in my speaking,
God in my thinking.

God in my sleeping,
God in my waking,
God in my watching,
God in my hoping.

God in my life,
God in my lips,
God in my hands,
God in my heart.

God in my sufficing,
God in my slumber,
God in mine ever-living soul,
God in mine eternity.

(Carmichael, 1983)

The Celtic pilgrim held together the paradox that this world is not our home, yet it is God's world and he has given it to us. If we are not content with what God has given us, why should we ask him for another world? Though guests and pilgrims of the world and strangers upon the earth, we are asked to love the world with the great love that God has for the world. God so loved the world that he gave himself for it (see John 3.16), and he wants us to give ourselves for it also. Celtic pilgrims saw themselves as building up God's kingdom now on earth; they set out to win the world back to God. There was a belief that everything was basically good, though it had been tainted and perverted by evil, and had to be restored by our work to its Maker. They would pray, 'Your kingdom come, your will be done in earth as it is in heaven', and they would work towards that end. The setting up of their monastic cities was with the ideal of making them places where God's will is done and therefore places of his kingdom here on earth. Their settlements were to be cities of God.

It is on this earth we are called to serve God and worship him with all our hearts and mind. It is on this earth we are called to seek his face. To turn away from God is to enter into darkness and die, so we have to set our face towards our God.

> I have turned back to you
> and ask you to give me the means to draw
>   close to you.
> If you leave us we die!
> But you will not leave us, because you are
>   wholly good,
> and do not let a sincere heart seek you
>   without finding you.

> (Augustine of Hippo)
> (Boldoni, 1987, p. 4)

Brendan knew no one can see God and live. He had been to the Land of Promise. He had obeyed God's will as best he could all his life; he had been allowed this special visit because his life on earth was coming to an end and he was being called home. Like many people, before his death, Brendan has had a glimpse of the glory which is ahead of him.

Brendan's community was rapturous with joy at his return, and glorified God for his kindness in letting them once more enjoy the sight of their father from whom they had been separated so long. Brendan returned their affection and recounted everything he remembered of the voyage and all the wonders God deigned to show him. Finally he informed them of the prophecy made by the young man on the island of Promise, assuring them that he had not long to live. Events proved him right: he put all his affairs in order, and very shortly afterwards, fortified with the sacraments of the Church, lay back in the arms of his disciples and gave up his illustrious spirit to the Lord, to whom be honour and glory, world without end. Amen.

(Webb, 1983, p. 245)

There was no sadness in this departure, rather it was a time of joy, for Brendan was going home to the God he had sought to serve all his life and he would enter fully into the Land of Promise, the kingdom of God. Some words of Dag Hammarskjöld could well fit Brendan's parting:

With all the power of your body concentrated
    on the hand of the tiller,
All the power of your mind concentrated on
    the goal beyond the horizon,

116

You laugh as the salt spray catches your face
    in the second of rest
Before a new wave –
Sharing the happy freedom with those who
    share your responsibility.
So – in the self-forgetfulness of concentrated
    attention –
the door opens for you into pure living
    intimacy.
A shared timeless happiness,
Conveyed by a smile,
A wave of the hand.
Thanks to those who have taught me this.
    Thanks to the days which have taught
    me this.

(Hammarskjöld, 1964, p. 90)

Obviously for Brendan death was not the end; it was the beginning of a greater adventure. What he had longed for and worked for he would now see and know. Due to the shared efforts of fellow workers and worshippers, he was now moving with confidence to his home with God.

I used to travelled by bus to Newcastle to see my future wife, Denise. On this journey the conductor used to say, 'We are coming to the end of the journey, to the terminus, this is where you all get off.' There was a finality in his words, suggesting no one could go any further, and yet not one of us would stay in the terminus; the end of this journey was the beginning of another. The terminus itself often looked dull and a little frightening but no one would stay there. They would move on, in my case I looked forward with great anticipation. I knew that for me, 'Journeys end in lovers meeting' (*Twelfth Night*, Act 2, Scene 3). And so it is when we come to that terminus called death, our Loved One is calling us home, and to the fullness of his kingdom. Often Denise would meet me at the terminus. I then did not notice how dull and frightening it was, only her presence. Let it be the same when we meet with our God at the last.

The Celtic Christians of the Hebrides asked God to meet them at their homecoming:

> When the soul separates
> From the perverse body,
> And goes in bursts of light
> Up from out of its human frame,
> Thou holy God of eternity,
> Come to seek me and to find me.
>
> May God and Jesus aid me,
> May God and Jesus protect me,
> May God and Jesus eternally
> Seek me and find me.
> (Carmichael, 1983, p. 350)

The God who journeys with us all our days will not leave us at the last. He who has guided us through every strait will shield us in the hour of our death and bring us home. Again the Hebridean Christian would pray:

> O God give me, of thy wisdom,
> O God give me, of thy mercy,
> O God give me, of thy fullness,
> And of thy guidance in face of every strait.
>
> O God give me, of thy holiness,
> O God give me, of thy shielding,
> O God give me, of thy surrounding,

And of thy peace in the knot of death.
Oh give me, of thy surrounding,
And of thy peace in the knot of death!
(Carmichael, 1976, p. 375)

As at the beginning of the journey so at its end. All of
life is an adventure, a reaching out and an extending
of ourselves; in our God nothing, no one is lost. We
will be called to leave behind our present securities
and position, our knowledge of what lies ahead and
our earthly wealth. If life does this to us more than
once, it could be seen as a preparation for the last
journey. We know, through the love of God, that death
is not the end:

So God our pilgrimage impels,
To cross sea-waste or scale life-fells;
A further shore,
One hill brow more,
Draws on the feet, or arm-plied oars,
As the soul onward, upward soars.

Beyond the hills a wider plain,
Beyond the waves the Isle Domain
With richness blest
And place for guest,
Where God doth sit upon his throne,
The soul by Christ nor left alone.
(McLean, 1961, p. 55)

EXERCISES

PAUSE

Each day make a homecoming and return to your
God. This turning may begin with a confession of sin

and penitence. It may be that we have wandered so far we are not sure where to turn. Know that as soon as you turn your Father comes to meet you. It is God who has called you and has been waiting for you. God welcomes you with open heart and open arms. Say to yourself, allowing each word to have impact:

> I will arise
> and go to my Father
> and say I have sinned before heaven and
> before you and am not worthy . . .

Then let God accept you into his Presence and to enfold you in his love. Rest in the peace, in the power and in the presence of God who is Almighty. Let God renew, refresh and restore you. When you have no power in yourself, know that all power belongs to God. As you rest in His love say:

> Still me, O Lord, as you stilled the storm.
> Calm me, O Lord, and keep me from harm.
> Let all the troubles within me cease.
> Enfold me, Lord, in your peace.

PRAY

Heed these words from St Augustine:

Do not be afraid
to throw yourself on the Lord!
He will not draw back
and let you fall!
Put your worries aside and throw yourself on him:
he will welcome you and heal you.

(Adam, 1985)